T0128861

Includes practical resource checklists
to help guide you through the process

BUSINESS
EXIT
COMPANION

*An Owner's Guide to Exit Planning
and Unlocking Value*

KOOS KRUGER

BUSINESS EXIT COMPANION
An Owner's Guide to Exit Planning and Unlocking Value

iUniverse books may be ordered through booksellers or by contacting:

iUniverse
1663 Liberty Drive
Bloomington, IN 47403
www.iuniverse.com
1-800-Authors (1-800-288-4677)

ISBN: 978-1-4917-6910-2 (sc)
ISBN: 978-1-4917-6911-9 (e)

Library of Congress Control Number: 2015911872

Print information available on the last page.

iUniverse rev. date: 09/24/2015

DISCLAIMER

This book aims to give the reader an overview of how to build and enact a transition and exit plan. This book is prepared solely for educational and information purposes. The author and publisher are not offering it as legal, accounting, or other professional services advice. The advice provided is general advice only. It has been written without taking into account the objectives, financial situations, or needs of the reader. Before acting on the advice, you should consider the appropriateness of the content, having regard to your own objectives, financial situation, and needs.

While best efforts have been used in preparing this book, the author and publisher make no representations or warranties of any kind and assume no liabilities of any kind with respect to the accuracy or completeness of the contents and specifically disclaim any implied warranties of merchantability or fitness of use for a particular purpose. Neither the author nor the publisher shall be held liable or responsible to any person or entity with respect to any loss or incidental or consequential damages caused, or alleged to have been caused, directly or indirectly, by the information or resources contained herein. No warranty may be created or extended by sales representatives or written sales materials. Every company is different, and the advice and strategies contained herein may not be suitable for your situation. You should seek the services of a competent professional before beginning any transition and exit-planning process. The content of the book is no substitute for professional advice.

To my incredible, unbelievable family:
Davina, Linze, Ashton and Chelsea

CONTENTS

ABOUT THE AUTHOR

Koos Kruger assists clients through his consulting companies, helping businesses with practical solutions to solve complex business problems in an easy manner. *Business Exit Companion* specializes in business advice and exit-planning services for business owners of small/medium businesses. *Krusner Business Services* delivers transformation and change management service to large corporates, including Rio Tinto, Downer EDI, Serco, and NSW government.

Koos has more than twenty-five years of progressive experience in management, finance, and operations. A chartered accountant with a proven history of growing both top and bottom lines of businesses, he has a broad industry background in health care, construction, financial services, manufacturing, fast-moving consumable goods, and professional services.

Koos was born in Johannesburg, South Africa, and began his career as a chartered accountant at KPMG in 1986, working with small to medium-size businesses, helping many entrepreneurs with the success of their businesses.

In the mid-1990s, he moved into the multinational corporate setting as a finance executive working for SAB Miller and Standard Bank, where he led many large-scale transformation projects, including the implementation of SAP in both organizations.

Koos moved back to KPMG as director responsible for one of their consulting practices. Over a two-year period, he quadrupled the size of the business, and some of his clients included HSBC, BHP Billiton, Allianz Insurance, Munich Re, Nedlloyd, and South African government.

Koos moved to Sydney, Australia, in 2004, where he currently lives with his wife, Davina, and three children, Linze, Ashton and Chelsea.

FOREWORD

Koos Kruger leaned across my desk and sketched a back-to-front business graph, which instantly unlocked an enigma I had about exiting my business.

All is explained in this book, *Business Exit Companion*.

"Which comes first, the chicken or the egg?" and "Don't put the cart before the horse" are both well-known expressions drummed into me from an early age. I was always told to start from the beginning, crawl before you walk, learn to draw first if you want to be an artist. All are true but miss a vital point that should be included ... the ending.

When you're an artist, what is your plan? When and how will you stop painting?

When people asked me what I was going to do when I retired, I would reply, "Paint of course" (God gifted me with this talent). "It's the only career that has no use-by date, even when you die!" I would say with a smug smile.

The mistake I had made, until I met Koos, was believing exiting a business and retiring from a business were one and the same.

Only then did I realize I had two very close and very successful business friends with classic examples that demonstrated to me exiting and retiring are as different as a donkey and a fox.

For the sake of keeping two dear friends and long-time mentors, I have changed their names and businesses.

Every time I visited Bill and his wife, Jane, at their nice but average retirement home on the Central Coast of New South Wales, Jane would grab an opportune moment to take me aside and tell me that Bill was getting worse, suffering from depression, fatigue, dementia, even early stages of Alzheimer's and bouts of anger like nothing she had seen before.

"I just don't know what to do, and he won't see a doctor," she said.

This puzzled me, as Bill had retired from his enormously successful medical practice and could get any amount of doctor's advice or treatment he would ever need.

Bill was always in my top-ten rich list, and when I was with him, none of the symptoms Jane was describing were coming to light. I just put it down to the fact they were adjusting to downsizing from their seven-bedroom family home with tennis court, pool, and harbor views, now that all their kids had left home.

However, something was radically wrong, as the picture just didn't fit. It was only when Bill and I went for a walk along the beach one day that he confided in me what was really wrong. "Jane thinks I've got chronic depression, dementia, and all those terrible things, but

I haven't," he said. "I've had every test and scan possible, and it was finally an old doctor mate that diagnosed me correctly," he said.

The doctor had said to him, "Bill, the only thing wrong with you is that you didn't plan for your retirement."

Bill said to me, "John, if I can give you one bit of advice, plan how to get out of your business starting now … this very minute! I thought my medical business would go on forever, and I would be still running it from my beach house well into my eighties, but I was bought out for virtually nothing, and Jane and I are on the pension. We're just okay, but we have to cut our cloth very carefully."

It dawned on me that I was heading down the same track, believing that I could paint forever and that all would be fine. What I realized was that Bill was bored out of his mind, didn't have hobbies he loved, and had no hope for the future except a trip to the happy hunting ground. I realized that I had to get an identity outside my business and that it was more than just painting.

My second friend is the exact opposite.

Bob and his wife, Alice, are retired. They travel the world, own three homes, have a hobby farm, ski lodge, beach house, yacht, cruiser, and an array of high-risk fun investments like restaurants, interior design shops, and a vintage car restoration garage.

It seems they can't help but to get richer the more time they spend in retirement.

I had the fortune to work for Bob some twenty-five years ago. He had a very successful car dealership in the western suburbs of Sydney, and he had a plan to combine with dealerships in the eastern suburbs and North Shore to be one mega dealership.

After working on this concept with him, I couldn't see how it was going to benefit Bob, other than giving him a bigger ego but with a lot more worry. I asked him point blank, "Why are you doing this?" His expression went deadpan, and he said in almost a whisper, "It's my way out."

Bob went ahead, and the combined dealership was formed and is still market-share leader today. However, in what appeared to be nothing short of a rocket-blast start just three years after forming the company, Bob at the age of fifty-six suddenly resigned and retired.

Whether he planned to exit then, decided he'd had enough, or even was railroaded out, I'll never know. But what I do know is he was ready with an exit plan to trigger at the right moment for him.

He also has repeatedly said to me, "If ever you're faced with a business conflict, don't let your would-be attacker know that you are going to hit them first."

From what Bob said, I believe an exit plan is like a concealed weapon at the ready. Every person in business should carry one at all times, and only those closest to that person know he or she has it. Most people get to the end of their working career and hope to sell their business. Many do so with little success and then have no idea what's next. They are just retiring. Those with an exit plan have a clear strategy as to what will happen with their business the day they stop working and already started working on the transition from full-time work to life after work.

Koos Kruger repeatedly in this book makes reference to recruiting your inner circle who can advise and support you in readiness, if and when you have to use your exit plan.

An exit or end strategy should be the beginning of any business venture. When you think about it, an exit or end strategy is the foundation to almost everything in our daily lives. A football match doesn't start with the kickoff and go forever. A play, novel, and film are all created with the end in mind before it is started, which is the most secretive part.

"You must see this play. I won't spoil it by telling you the ending." How many times have you heard similar statements to that?

In this book, Koos Kruger gives the insight and structure on how to go about creating your very own exit plan. A must-read for any business owner/partner.

That very first meeting where Koos Kruger leaned across my desk and drew that simple business graph was to become my Get out of Jail card. After developing an exit plan for me, within twelve months and with his caring, professional advice, Koos had led me out of a steep financial nosedive to exiting the IVF business I founded eight years prior, cleanly and well rewarded. My exit plan helped me to avoid going down the same path as Bill, and I am now enjoying life like Bob explained to me many years ago.

I am forever grateful for meeting and working with Koos Kruger.

John Brain, Business Owner and Artist

INTRODUCTION

*Give me six hours to chop down a tree, and I will
spend the first four sharpening my axe.*

—Abraham Lincoln

This practical guide is designed to be your companion to help you along your business exit-planning journey. The useful resources at the end of each chapter are both a summary of the chapter and an effective tool to guide all business owners.

What is a transition and exit plan, you ask? In simple terms, it is a comprehensive road map to successfully exit a privately held business and prepare the owner for life after work. It asks and answers all the business, personal, family, financial, legal, and tax questions involved in exiting a privately owned business. It includes contingencies for illness, burnout, divorce, and even an owner's death.

Its purpose is to maximize the value of the business at the time of exit, minimize the amount of taxes paid, and ensure that the business owner is able to accomplish all his or her personal and financial goals in the process.

The failure to create a well-defined plan in my experience virtually guarantees that business owners will:

- exit their businesses as a result of pressure from outside circumstances, not as a result of their own desires
- exit their businesses on a timetable that's forced on them instead of one that meets their needs
- undervalue their business and leave hard-earned wealth on the table
- pay too much in taxes
- lose control over the process by being reactive and limiting their exit options
- fail to realize all their business and personal goals
- suffer unnecessary psychological stress
- watch a lifetime of work disintegrate as a result of poor business continuity planning
- lose confidence during the sale or exit process

Planning ahead is valued but often not completed. Within your business life, it makes sense that you're more concerned about what's happening today instead of what's happening tomorrow. The benefit of planning ahead will allow you to concentrate more fully on the present business operations, a true benefit that can pay big dividends.

But tomorrow will come more quickly than you might expect.

The more you can plan for the future, the more you can focus on the present day, allowing you to build the success your organization deserves—and that you and your family deserve.

Remember, this transition affects more than just you, and it impacts more than just what you will do when you're not going to work anymore. This transition from working to not working is something that must be carefully orchestrated, planned, and organized.

You need a comprehensive plan. You need a way to ensure you're heading in the right direction—long before you get there. You also need the time to execute the plan and build the resources that will ensure you can enjoy your retirement.

Building an exit plan for you and your business is more than just counting down until the day you sell your company or the day you retire. It's a comprehensive plan for getting what you want from your company as well as what you deserve.

In this book, you will move through six different chapters, each with information that builds on the previous chapter to help you create the best possible plan—no matter what your goals.

- Chapter 1 offers background as to what you need to plan and why, and it provides you tools to assess where you are at presently.
- Chapter 2 explains all the resources you need to prepare the exit plan.
- Chapter 3 helps you understand what your business is worth now and explains how you can maximize its value. Your business is one of the biggest assets you have, if not the biggest asset. How do you know what it is worth now, and how can you maximize the value?
- Chapter 4 provides fourteen steps and ideas to improve the value of your business.

- Chapter 5 identifies the money aspects of what you will need when you get to retirement.
- Chapter 6 explains the steps you need to take to transition from full-time work to the new life you have planned for yourself.

The checklists and questionnaires contained within each chapter are designed to help you along the journey to exiting your business to retirement or other ventures. You will get the best value out of these checklists if you are as honest with yourself as possible. Low scores indicate areas that you would need to pay further attention to as part of planning your exit, or where you need the support of an expert adviser. Refer to each chapter of the book for more details on the items contained in the checklists.

There's no time like the present to begin building your plan. You can begin today and start changing the way you look at your future.

Formulating a precise exit plan for your businesses won't minimize the chance of unexpected bumps in the road. Those bumps will come no matter what you do. However, having a structured exit plan can help you better navigate your businesses in the present, thereby maximizing the chance that you can view the future with more peace of mind. With more peace of mind and more concentration on your present business, you are better able to deal with the inevitable obstacles and challenges that emerge as any business evolves.

This book is written for every person that owns a business, either as a sole trader or as a partner, within a large or small business, to get you to think about what your future will look like and to take action now on how you are going to get there.

Tomorrow might be too late, as many retired business owners will confess.

WHAT YOU NEED TO KNOW

Begin with the end in mind.
—Stephen R. Covey

In this chapter, we will discuss the idea of planning for your exit and the following components of exit planning:

1. Retirement planning
2. Financial planning
3. Estate planning
4. Business planning
5. Tax planning
6. Exit strategy
7. Succession planning

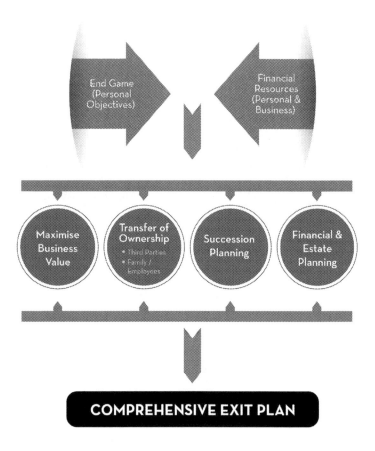

With this information, you will have the foundation for working within the planning process of moving from *thinking* about leaving your company to being 100 percent ready.

We will also cover the basics of what kinds of businesses should consider exit planning, what happens when families are involved, and how small-business owners need to have a strategy in place. Every business and every business owner or leader deserves to have an exit plan in place. What kind you will need may vary, but a plan is the best way to prepare everyone for the inevitable future.

Often I find business owners having a well-documented retirement plan in place and very confident that it is all they need. As you will soon discover, exit planning is more than just thinking about what your retirement will look like; it is thinking about all the aspects of your business and family. It also looks at how to maximize the value of your business and ensure its success after you have left the business.

When you're in business for yourself, it can seem as though you're in the middle of a battlefield at times. Not only are you trying to manage the everyday needs of your company but you're also in charge of the long-term goals.

Though you may try to keep every aspect of your business in mind, this isn't always possible. Or you may believe your company will simply continue on long after you leave.

In other words, not everyone plans for the future. It is often the unforeseen events, or the three Ds (death, divorce, or disease), that most business owners are faced with, resulting in an exit from their business that is unplanned with nothing in place to manage the process.

If you're one of those people, you need to think about this approach and reconsider your position. After all, when you don't plan for the days to come, you may end up unhappy with what happens.

You may set up the future owners of your company for failure, or you might not plan for your retirement, leaving your family without the support they need.

Your business and its future aren't just about you. You need to think bigger, and that begins with thinking about what might happen in the days when you won't be around to help.

What happens if the unforeseen occurs and you have to exit much earlier than you thought you would retire? Who knows what tomorrow will bring? You can only be sure you are prepared if you have a plan.

To continue to motivate you to begin your exit planning and strategy, let's talk about what your *why* is. Many people will focus on the *what* of the planning process, which makes sense, but if you're not thinking about the why, then you may not take the direction you actually want to take.

You knew why you started your business, and now it's time to figure out why you would want to leave the business.

Is it age?

It is common for people who are over forty to begin to think about the next stage of life and their role in it. They begin to wonder if they are ready to move on or if they might be able to retire early.

If this sounds like you, you may also be thinking about if you might try something new in your career, especially if you're younger.

Consider your age and what that means to you. After all, there's nothing saying you can't start a new business when you're over fifty. The average life expectancy in most developed countries is between eighty and eighty-five years, so there could still be a good fifteen to twenty years before you decide to slow down.

Is it money?

For others, the why of the exit-planning process might be related directly to financial goals. You may want to stop working or you may want to sell your company in order to use the money for a specific reason.

You may also know that your company is more valuable than it might be at any other time. So, the decision to exit may be based on taking advantage of the higher value and position.

Consider what your money goals are, and then you can use the planning process to meet these goals.

Is it time?

For some, the timing of exit planning is simply related to the idea of retirement. They just want to retire and be done with working. Even if this isn't connected to the customary age that a person might retire, you might have a sense that it's time for someone else to be in charge and run the show.

You may have had an idea in your head for a while about when you were going to retire and step back from your role.

Are others pressuring you?

In other situations, it might be that others are prodding you to leave or pressuring you to think about leaving. While this may not have been a conversation that started with you, it is a conversation that may get you thinking.

After all, an outside perspective of your role in the company might be helpful to show you what the company might need.

That said, pressure from outsiders should be something that you consider alongside your own motivations, instead of just giving into the thoughts of another.

In the end, the why might be as simple as wanting to have something else in your life. You may have been in your company for decades and feel you are being called somewhere else.

This is a valid reason to want to move into another company or to simply exit this company.

In the end, it comes down to: What do you want? Why do you want to exit? Is this the right time?

And only you can answer those questions.

To make sure you're making a decision that's based on facts instead of emotions, it's best to:

1. Figure out the *why* and *what* you want life to look like after the exit.
2. Start with *where* you are.
3. Learn about the *how.*
4. Decide on *what* you will do.
5. See *who* can help.

The more you can make this a collaborative process, the better. Find people who are outside of the realm of benefitting from your exit, as you want to gather unbiased opinions and options.

THE BENEFITS OF PLANNING

It is common sense to plan ahead, but even while this is true, that doesn't mean everyone does it. If you need more motivation and more reasons to start you're planning now, here's what you need to keep in mind: There are only four avenues where your money can go when you exit your business. You can use it to fund the new lifestyle you choose, or you may decide to give some to your family and charities, or depending on how well you have planned, some and often a lot will need to go to pay taxes. All these avenues for where your money can go will be covered in more detail later in the book.

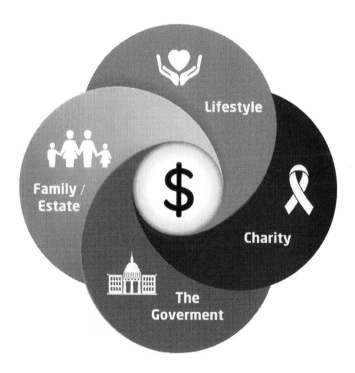

With a plan in place, you can ensure your money is directed where you want it to go.

As a business owner, you have a lot on your mind every day. You know you need to provide for your employees and your team. But what about you? Planning your exit is all about you, your needs, and your family. (And that's probably why many business owners avoid thinking about it.)

It doesn't always seem right to think about the end when you're still in business. For some, this might feel as though you're simply trying to get out of your work and your responsibilities.

But planning is essential for your business to thrive—and for you to thrive.

When you have a plan in place, you'll be able to:

- *Do the things you want to do.* The truth is that many people want to exit their businesses because they want to move on to something else. They may want to switch professions, or they may want to simply sit on a beach and enjoy their later years. When you have a plan in place, you can ensure you will be doing what you want to do when you sell your business or you retire.
- *Get the most for your company.* The more you can plan ahead, the more likely you will be to get the most from your company. If you simply decide to sell your company without any planning, you may not have the systems or processes or talent in place to position your company as having a higher value.
- *Control your timing.* If you're not planning ahead, you may not have control over the timing of your exit (and that may mean you aren't completely ready for what will happen next in your life). If you want to be in control, you need to be the one who writes the plan.
- *Ensure your financial security.* While you may not worry about your financial security now, if you want to retire early, for example, you will need to have the money ready for you to

spend. This process of planning can take time and needs careful thought.

- *Keep business/family relations intact.* As you create a succession plan for your business, early planning will help everyone be a part of the decision making, which can soothe any possible problems along the way. After all, you can't quite get rid of your family, so they should be a part of the process too.

- *Reduce uncertainty.* No matter what your business's future may look like to you, your staff and other employees need to know they are going to be okay when you leave. With a plan, you will ensure they understand they are still going to have a job.

- *Know your options.* While you can certainly exit your business quickly, you may not understand all your options when you leave in a quick manner. Instead, planning ahead will allow you to review and consider every single option you have, allowing you to think things through before you have to make a decision.

- *Minimize taxes/other fees.* It costs money to change the way a business is run or owned. But you can offset those costs with the help of a tax professional. However, it's easier to plan ahead than to simply cross your fingers and hope you don't owe too much when you sell or transfer your business.

- *Protect the long-term value of your business.* You've spent time, energy, and money building your business. Instead of simply exiting your company and hoping for the best, planning will help you ensure your company is ready for the future and that it will continue to hold value for customers and team members.

Not surprisingly, there is a long list of benefits to planning anything. The more you consider the value of planning, the more you will be inspired to get started.

For those who are still not convinced, there are problems that can and will happen when you put off or avoid planning. Like the saying goes, "When you fail to plan, you plan to fail". Even if you don't have a plan in place, you will still be affected by that lack of a plan.

Some of the downsides to not planning include the following:

- *Undervaluing your company.* When you don't plan ahead, you can't get the most value for your company. You will only get what you can get at the time of the sale.
- *Paying too much in capital gains or taxes, etc.* The taxes and other payments you don't plan for will fall on you at the time of your exit, or they will fall on your family if you have died.
- *Not playing an active role in the exit process.* Often, when there is no exit plan in place, you cannot guide the process once it begins. Things may happen around you, or other team members may create the plan for you.
- *Not being in control of what happens to your company.* You have spent years building up your business, and that means you should be able to control what happens next. Without a plan, you will not be in control. Even if you are making decisions, you will be making them in reaction to other events, not guiding the process.
- *Not being able to have the financial security you expected.* When you create a business, you need to know your financial future is set, even when you exit. Your family is counting on you, but without a plan, you may not be able to have that security you expected. You may have to continue to work, exit later than you planned, or find another source of revenue.
- *Creating a burden on your family.* Though no one wants to think about dying, it will happen at some point. If you don't create a plan for that type of exit, then your family may be left with making decisions they don't understand, making payments

they didn't account for, and managing a business that wasn't prepared for your exit.

Of course, the less you plan, the more problems you will see (or your family or partners will see). Planning is important no matter the size of your business, even for small businesses.

SMALL BUSINESSES

For a long time, it seemed as though owners of small businesses would never need to worry about exit planning. The business would simply close when the boss decided to leave. Though this seems abrupt (and still is), the owners of these companies weren't necessarily in charge of a lot of people, and they may have been more niche in nature, meaning they weren't necessarily in the larger market.

But this is not the situation anymore.

Today, small businesses might:

- be bought by another company
- be taken over by a long-time employee
- grow into a larger business

Since there are more options today, owners of small businesses should consider creating a plan for what might happen after an owner or partner leaves.

Owners of small businesses who might be interested in being bought out need to figure out how to prepare for this situation and how they will manage the transition.

The world has changed, and while a small company might be small in its location or product selection, it can still be a part of the larger global market. It can still be profitable and successful, which can attract the attention of an investor or another company.

In that case, it's clear that small-business owners need to complete exit planning too, often for the following reasons:

- *You have more customers to care for.* When you have a website and/or an online store, you're talking to a larger market, a market in which you can have more customers than in the past. As a result, your company serves a need that requires a clear transition plan for your exit from the leadership team.
- *You have more employees.* Even if you don't have a lot of employees in one location, you might have more staff members in your operation, though off-site. To ensure everyone on the team is covered and cared for during a transition, you need to plan for your exit (and for the exits of other key team members).
- *Your idea needs to be supported.* What you may forget about your small business is that you were the one who came up with the brilliant idea. You were the one who came up with the thing that made customers excited to come to your store. But if you're not there, and you don't plan for someone to have your knowledge-set, then the company may not see the same results as it did with you around.

Small business owners often think they don't have to work as hard since they're not as big. While it's true you may not have as many people in the decision-making processes, you also need to remember how you impact the company as a whole. One person's departure can have a large impact.

You are, right now, in the place of considering how you need to plan and what strategy you need to have in place to meet your needs.

But you can't know where to go unless you know where you are right now. The first thing to consider is the type of company you have.

WHAT KIND OF COMPANY DO YOU HAVE?

Whether you're a smaller company or a company that has hundreds of employees, exit planning is still the key to your long-term success.

In a private company with more than one owner, you need to consider the exit plans of the other owners and ensure that there is agreement on aspects like business planning, exit strategy, and succession planning. In a family company, there are more team members than just you to consider, as discussed in the next section.

Assessing your company now is an ideal starting point. This might be a time to see what your company is doing, what its value is, and what its structure includes.

Make an inventory of your company as it is right now and try to understand how it is structured in relation to the rest of the business world.

You might include a list of information that details:

- services/products
- number of employees
- organizational flowchart
- current financials
- market research

While some business owners who are thinking about an exit strategy think more about how they are simply going to leave, you may want more for your company.

If this is the case, you need to understand where you are. You will do this by looking at your exit readiness and asking questions about whether your company is ready.

- Is your family ready?
- Are you ready?

We'll go over these questions in more detail later in the book. The next thing to understand before you plan is where you find yourself right now.

WHERE ARE YOU NOW?

Most of us are so caught up in the every day that we don't stop to take a breath, much less stop to consider why we're doing what we're doing. But when you're planning for the future, you need to ask these questions, and you need to make sure you're doing a little navel gazing, since this is a decision that will impact the rest of your life.

Actually, it's a series of decisions that will impact you and those around you.

The questions that follow will help outline where the business is and where it might be going next. Some of the questions can be answered by everyone, but others will need to be answered by you. The more you can bring everyone into the conversation with you, the easier the entire process will be.

(But it can also help for you to answer these questions for yourself before you sit down with anyone else. Know what you want so you're not necessarily swayed by what others want.)

BUSINESS

- Who might take over your responsibilities?
- What will happen to your employees?
- Will the company still be in operation if you are not around?
- Who legally owns the business?
- What is the market outlook?
- Is there a plan for the business?
- Who could buy your business?

FINANCIAL

- What is your financial position?
- How much will you make from the exit?
- How much money do you need?
- How much money do you want from the exit?
- How will the money be distributed?

LEGAL

- What contracts do you have in place?
- What contracts need to be in place?
- What legal arrangements are required during the transition?
- What does your legal team suggest?

PERSONAL

- What do you want to do after you exit?
- What are you going to do in your free time?
- What happens to your family if the unforeseen happens?
- What do you need to support your family?

TAXES

- What taxes do you owe?
- What taxes will you owe?
- How can you reduce your taxes?

VALUE CREATION

- How much is the company worth today?
- How can you boost the value of your company?
- What value creation efforts are already working?
- What value creation efforts are not working?

When you begin to ask these questions, you will no doubt come up with other questions to answer as well. It's the nature of planning—to continue to see what *else* you need to do.

Everything you learn can bring up what you don't already know and what you need to know soon.

Now that you have a better picture of where you are, it's time to start focusing on the plan itself. Let's learn more about the how.

EXIT-PLANNING PROCESS

The exit-planning process looks different for everyone, but the strategic approach follows the same outline. A comprehensive exit plan should at least cover these seven core elements:

1. Mental and financial readiness (retirement planning)
2. Money (financial planning)
3. Family (estate planning)
4. Maximize the business's value (business planning)
5. Financial obligations (tax planning)

6. The new owner (exit strategy)
7. Key employees (succession planning)

1. RETIREMENT PLANNING

The financial readiness part of the plan considers what you will need for your finances. You begin to consider the planning that needs to be done, and you might begin to worry whether you'll ever be ready for the eventual exit.

The mental readiness of an exit plan isn't often considered. Owners have to leave their businesses eventually, but not everyone is ready for it when the day comes. When you're not ready for the transition, it might cause you to make decisions in the exit plan and strategy that aren't conducive to the results you want to see.

Of course, you may have already started to think about retirement long before it's time for you to actually take this step. In retirement planning, you're starting to figure out what you will want and what you're going to do when you actually stop going to work every day.

Since retirement means you won't be getting a regular paycheck, you need to make sure you're taking time to best understand what you need to have around to support yourself and your family. You begin to think about what you need to fund this part of your life and your career (even though you're stepping away from your career).

In many cases, people may not think this through, as they believe their pension or their savings will sustain them. While this might be true for some, if you're not positive this is the case, it's time to start planning ahead. You need to make sure that every possibility is considered, as well as every expense and every cost you might incur in the coming years.

Though it might seem far away, retirement preparation is something that can take years. The earlier you begin, the more effective the outcome will be for your future plans.

While it may sound simple, retirement planning gets complicated when you factor in more than funds. Let's do a quick assessment. The following questions will help us focus on the key areas of consideration:

- *What do I need?* The money you need and the resources you need are the things to list first. The more you can understand the breadth of your needs and your goals, the more you can put into place plans and strategies that will drive you toward your goals.
- *What do others need?* Sometimes, it's not just about you, and it's not just about what you want to have in place. You may have a family, or you might anticipate having a family to support. The more you can provide for them now, the more you can

do when you're still around. In addition, you might want to think about how many people you want to support during your retirement. You may want to help out your children, your grandchildren, or other loved ones. Make sure everyone is on your list as being a part of your retirement planning.

- *What do I already have?* If you have a pension or other funds already in place, get clarity about what this means and how it might change the way you save. Determine the best course of action when it comes to filling in the gap between what you need and what you already have.

- *What happens when I retire?* Though you might already have a clear idea of what retirement looks like, not everyone does. Consider what happens and what your life will look like when you don't go into the office anymore. Take the example off Bill, as described in the foreword, who had a successful career as a medical practitioner. He retired without a clear plan of what life would look like after retirement, leaving him feeling adrift after leaving the medical profession. Soon he found himself depressed and not enjoying his retirement, causing not only himself but also his wife to suffer deeply.

The more detailed you can be in your planning, the more effective you will be. Be sure to plan for every possible contingency, and you will do the very best you can for yourself and for your family. Contingencies to consider include a downturn in the financial market, placing pressure on your finances (e.g., the low interest rates globally resulting in lower interest earned), long-term illness that changes the life you have planned and sometimes even where you planned to live, or a change in the circumstance of a child, causing you to step in and help.

Retirement planning should begin as soon as possible, even as soon as you start your business. When you begin early, you have a longer period to accumulate savings, benefit from the impact of compound interest, and handle any problems in your saving plan along the way (i.e., stock market crashes, unexpected financial needs).

Though everyone's retirement plan will look different, these are the basic steps to planning for that time when the only thing you're in charge of is what you want to do each day.

We will explore these issues in much more detail in chapter 5, "Money Matters."

2. FINANCIAL PLANNING

When it comes to your finances, you can't simply hope that your savings will sustain you—at least, this isn't the case for most.

Since you can't determine just how long you will live and what the quality of your life might be, you need to start planning on more than just taking money from your accounts.

You need to start considering your investment strategy. Depending on where you are in your career and your work history, you might choose to have a riskier investment strategy versus a safer investment strategy. Chapter 5 discusses investment risk in more detail.

In either case, you still need to have a strategy in place. You still need to have some sort of plan that will help you manage your finances and keep your long-term goals sustainable.

The more you prepare now, the more effective the strategies will be, even if the markets don't perform the way you expect.

What you need to know is that the people who are able and willing to put their investment strategies into place early are the ones who see the most returns.

Your investment strategy should consider all these aspects:

- *What investments do I have?* Start with an assessment of what you already have in place and how those investments are performing.
- *What is my investment history*? It can be helpful to look at the past to see how you fared when you made investments. If you haven't seen positive results, it may be time to change your strategy or seek additional support.
- *What investments will I make?* Though you may not be able to answer this question succinctly or clearly at the present time, you will want to think about the types of investments available to you in your current financial state. Investments can range from low-risk term deposits to property or stocks, bonds, and commodities. The type of investment will be driven by the term of the investment (for example, property will be longer term in nature) and the risk you want to take with the investment (for example, term deposits have a guaranteed return but at a lower yield than other investment types where the return is not guaranteed).
- *How do I feel about risk?* Most financial planners would suggest that you pursue an aggressive investment strategy while you are young because you'll have longer to make up for losses through market rebounds and dollar cost averaging. As you move closer to retirement, the investments should be scaled back in terms of aggressive equities. But that's only if you lack sufficient cash flow from other sources to pay for retirement. If you have sufficient cash flow for retirement, then there's no reason to scale back on the aggressive nature of your investments because you will lose potential capital appreciation if you do.
- *How much help do I need?* If the thought of investing makes you nervous or confused, you should seek the assistance of a

competent financial adviser. The more help you have, either in the form of a financial adviser or a book on financial planning, the more guidance you will receive.

During the exit, you may also have money from the sale of your share, and this can cause its own conundrum. You will want to have a strategy in place for handling that money and using it wisely.

A large sum of money can lead to an emotional moment, one that might cause you to not use the money wisely. Have a strategy in place to make sure you're ready to use that money for your future dreams and a phenomenal tax liability.

Remember, there isn't one financial strategy that works for everyone. You will need to tailor your plan to your specific needs and goals.

Note: Financial planning also includes risk management in the form of insurances—life, trauma, permanent disability, and income protection. *What do I need if I die tomorrow and I have not reached my financial objectives?* (This is covered in chapter 5, "Money Matters.")

3. ESTATE PLANNING

Estate planning is something you may consider as outside of your business exit. But since you will probably be exiting to spend more time with your loved ones, you need to prepare for their future too, especially if you've been the one who has cared for them in the past.

While not directly linked to your wealth, a strong exit plan will include having some sort of outline for what happens to your estate once you are no longer around. It is truly amazing how many smart entrepreneurs neglect this very basic level of financial planning.

By planning this out, you ensure your family and loved ones aren't left to deal with any unforeseen financial complications.

Think about what might happen if you died before you retired. You may not want to think about it, but thinking this way will help you better understand what controls and plans you need to have in place. After all, if you were to die before all your financial strategies could play out, your family may be left to deal with the pieces.

With estate planning, you can begin to decide what happens to your estate (your land, your buildings, your property, etc.), as well as what might happen to your business if you're the owner of the company.

When you plan your estate and its movement after you die, you create a financial plan to handle taxes or other fees associated with transferring ownership. In addition, you will be able to leave your family and coworkers in a solid position. They won't have to make decisions that would be best made by you. You will already have made those decisions for them, and you will have ensured they can focus on their own lives and not on details they didn't expect to manage.

- *What do you own?* Take inventory of what you own and what you already have in your name. This might take more time than you realize, as you can own a lot over the course of a lifetime. You will want to talk with everyone in the company and in your family to see if there are things you own that you may not count or recall.
- *What do you share ownership of?* At the same time, you need to consider what you co-own with others. This will highlight areas in which you need to have conversations about what might happen to these co-owned pieces or properties.
- *What happens if you die before retirement?* No one wants to think about whether they will die before they retire, but if you

don't think about it, then you might miss out on opportunities to give your family and your business partners some peace of mind during an already troubling time.

Planning ahead is necessary, and the importance of a good plan cannot be overstated. An essential part of estate planning is procuring excellent legal advice. The up-front cost can be high, especially if you have significant assets and widespread familial obligations, but the investment is totally worth it. Also, estate plans evolve over time, so the initial plan should be revisited as circumstances change for good or ill.

4. BUSINESS PLANNING

If you own a business, you have to think about this when you're considering your exit planning. You need to think about how your business will be valued and how you might take steps now to increase its value.

When you are planning your exit from your business, it's important that you get the most from the company and your investments in the company. There are plenty of ways in which you can add value to a company during the implementation of the exit plan.

Even if you're not sure you want to sell your business right now, the more you consider the value of your company and its value in the future, the more you will be able to make decisions today that will have a positive impact tomorrow.

The key with this part of exit planning is that you need to remember that selling your business is just a part of the process. Since you are selling, you need to make sure you're getting the most you can from the sale, which means you need to be aware of the value of your business at all times.

Or you need to at least be aware of how you can determine the value of your business so you can also measure its health—both for today and tomorrow.

Since the sale of your business may become the money you have for your retirement or it might become the money that you use for other ventures, you need to be certain you have garnered all the money you can from it.

When you plan ahead for this to happen, you can look for opportunities to increase the value of your company. You can prepare your business to be in the best possible position when a prospective buyer comes along.

- *What is the value of my business now?* Consider what similar businesses in the market have sold for and what the future of your industry might look like. Valuing your business is covered in chapter 3.
- *What is the projected value of my business?* Think about how your business might look to investors and owners in the coming years. If your company is currently trendy, can you determine whether this popularity will continue in the future?
- *How can I increase the company's value*? When you're looking at the value of your company, and the number isn't what you want to see, you may need to find ways to increase its value. This could include looking at the competition to see how they are faring and whether there are improvements that need to be made right now. Chapter 4 provides fourteen steps to help improve the value of your business.
- *How can I set up the company for future success?* Even if you are selling the company and you won't be an active part of its future, you still need to make sure your company is ready for the future. In doing so, you will make the business more

attractive to buyers, and you will ensure that the company continues to provide for the new leadership and staff.

Planning for your business to succeed is something you've done since you started your business in the first place. But since you've started to look at the company as a way to settle your affairs and prepare for the future, you need to set up that plan now.

5. TAX PLANNING

Most people would rather ignore taxes, but avoiding tax planning can prove disastrous. The more you can look ahead at what the tax professionals will need from you and from your bank account, the more prepared you will be for your exit.

- *What taxes do I owe?* Even if you're currently up to date on your taxes, it can help to have a financial professional look over your books to see if you've missed something along the way. It might be that you have always been able to pay your taxes on time and accurately, but this is not the case for everyone.
- *What taxes result from selling a business, selling stocks, etc.?* Talk to a professional about what taxes you might incur when you start selling things or transitioning parts of your business to others. Since it might not be clear until you make these decisions, it's best to talk with someone who has handled these actions before.
- *What happens if I'm not around to pay my taxes?* Though this is hopefully not the case for you, there might be a situation in which you die before you can pay off taxes that you owe. In those cases, you might set aside some money for the taxes you would owe, and then another person or representative might be able to take those funds to settle your accounts. As a business owner, you should also make provision for estate taxes that will need to be paid by your heirs as part of the

assets you give to them in your will. You need to make sure that there will be funds for estate taxes to be paid.

- *What happens when I've done my taxes wrong?* You may not know about tax problems for a few years. As a result, you might get a bill that you didn't include in your retirement planning. Consider how you might be able to offset these tax surprises.

- *What taxes will I need to pay when I exit my business?* If you exit the business in the form of a sale of the business, you will be liable for capital-gain tax. This needs to be taken into account when planning how much money you will have from the sale of the business.

Taxes are confusing for most, which is often why professionals are called in during exit planning. Though this might not be the easiest part of your strategy or your plan, it is the part of the process that can cause the most trouble if it's avoided.

You don't want to have large amounts of taxes to deal with when you're in your retirement, and you certainly don't want your family or others to have to figure out ways to pay these taxes if you've died and are not around to manage them.

6. EXIT STRATEGY

If you don't know what you want, how can you strategize to make it happen? Just as in business, you need to clearly understand what is ahead of you and the steps you should (or could) take in order to get where you want to go. You need to do more than just think about your exit. You need to create a strategy or an actual plan that you will set into motion.

An exit strategy is a plan developed to extract the value of a business owner's investment in a business.

Common exit strategies for a privately owned business include:

- *Sale to a third party.* You might decide to sell your company to another party, helping to return money to you for your investment of time and energy (as well as money). Though this might not be possible in all cases, it is an option more companies are considering today.
- *Closing of the business or liquidation.* In some companies, it might be best to simply close the company when no one else in the family is interested in continuing on. For some, this is simply the best way to preserve the integrity of the company while also clearing the slate for new opportunities or for retirement.
- *Transfer to a family member.* Some family companies might opt to sell their company to a family member, preserving the ownership and the name of the organization. Often this transition has been carefully orchestrated in the years prior to the exit.
- *Sales to a management team.* If there is not a family member interested in purchasing the company or taking over ownership, the owner might sell the company to the management team. This offers the possibility of not having to stop the daily operations, and it also creates a time for new energy without significant changes to the brand.
- *Initial Public Offering (IPO).* For some companies, an IPO might be the way to create funding for a company, and possibly the accumulation of more funding than might be gathered from a traditional sale. At the same time, IPOs can be risky, as it's not always clear what will happen when you offer the company in a public sale of shares.

Each of these processes has its advantages. The more you look at each of the possibilities without any judgment or immediate response, the more you will be able to determine the best possible decision for you and your business.

You may find you have your eye fixed on one of these options, only to change your mind later.

7. SUCCESSION PLANNING

Another consideration is who will step into your shoes. This is the part of the plan where you consider who might take your place in the future and what the team might look like.

Succession isn't a simple, "Here are the keys, see you later," sort of transition. If you own a family-run business, there might be serious infighting among the relatives as a power play ensues, either before or after you leave. The same could go for moving someone from your team into the position of president and/or chief executive officer. So, as you plan for who will replace you, you need to consider the psychological and emotional implications. A key part of this is to make sure that you communicate to everyone involved so that they can understand why you are making the decisions you are making. Family matters are discussed in more detail in the next section.

When you have a solid team in place, this ensures a stable transition, no matter when you end up leaving your role.

If you're selling your business, you may be asked by the buyer to stay on for a transition period, or you may want to stay on to ensure your company is handled properly.

The employees you want to keep are next in the strategy's agenda. You may want to think about how the company could be set up to keep them, or how you can train newer employees to become the seasoned veterans when you leave.

Indeed, while you don't want to think of it, there might come a time when you are no longer there. Many business owners have passed away during their time at an organization, and some companies floundered because they didn't have a clear plan for who would take over in this instance.

You need to be ready at all times. And the perfect time to start is right now.

Succession isn't just about the development or the hiring of talent. You also need to think about how your company will move forward after you are gone.

Succession can be thought of as more than just a plan; it's a development process. In this process, you identify what the overall organizational chart might look like in your company (including people who may not have completely accurate titles for their roles).

With this information, you can see who will need to move into a new role when you leave. Then you can decide who might be the best candidate or candidates.

As you begin this process of planning and development, it can help to consider some new ideas in the business world about succession. Though you may not agree with these ideas, the more you consider all your options and the thoughts in this field, the more effective your decision making will be.

- The replacement doesn't have to be ready now.
- You don't have to find someone from the outside.

Though you will want to have someone on board who could take your place, there might be someone who is the emergency CEO, while someone else is the one you want in your position when you are gone.

The person that you want for your role should be someone who is:

- on his or her way to being right for the role
- invested in the job
- already preparing himself or herself for the job

You also need to consider how other people at the company feel about this person. While you may have the final say in who gets chosen for this role, if there are concerns from others, this placement may not be a good fit for the company.

Make sure that everyone is on board with this person, including the board and the leadership team. The more everyone is in consensus about the decision, the smoother the transition will be.

While many companies believe they should choose someone new and exciting to step into a departing leader's shoes, this is not always the best choice. Not only does this interrupt the organization and its team but it might also create a decrease in customer confidence. The clients you have will want to see the same team when you leave; this assures them that the company isn't changing too much.

All these things should begin to percolate in your head when you start the process of exit planning.

Everyone needs to work together as you begin the succession planning process. Ideally, you will get everyone's input regarding what the succession plan might look like.

In some companies, this might be a simple process of having people choose the individuals they would want in their roles. This creates an open conversation about how the company will move into the future. This takes away the concern about what happens next, and it creates opportunities for workers to train each other.

The mentoring process doesn't have to and shouldn't begin when you leave. In fact, this process should begin as soon as possible so that everyone is ready for the next phase in the company's life.

Developing someone begins with coming up with a plan that will enhance the notable skills he or she already has and that will increase his or her ability to move into the leadership role.

This might take on a mentoring quality. You might have the person work alongside you and step into your role when you are away, for example. It may be helpful for the person to have regular meetings with you to learn more about how you do what you do—and *why* you do what you do.

The more you create an ongoing relationship of development, the more the mentee will get from the process. And this is a process. Getting a person ready to step into your shoes is not something that should be done hastily. Instead, you want to make sure the person is not only ready but also prepared for the entire transition process.

Of course, during this process, you don't necessarily want to guarantee that this person will have the role. Unless you have things spelled out in a contract, it is a good idea not to promise anything.

Promising can sometimes lead to people not feeling they need to continue to impress you. If they already have the job, what is the incentive to work hard? True, the right person for the job will not feel like that or respond in that way.

Additionally, you need to remember that succession planning is about the long-term diversity of the organization. In today's times, you want to remember that diversity does matter in the eyes of others and in the eyes of the team members that haven't been hired yet.

Consider ways to make sure the mentoring process includes more diverse candidates for your job, as well as for the jobs that are below you.

To make succession planning interesting to those who are involved in the process, it can help to have people determine ways they can quantify their success. Perhaps this is a quantification of how many minority or women candidates they can develop or how many roles are filled with internal team members.

A succession plan can look like this:

- *Determine the skills needed.* For each role that might need to be filled when you leave or are gone, create a list of the skills, behaviors, attitudes, etc. This will help you and the rest of the leadership team begin to visualize who the perfect person for the job might be.
- *Know the direction of the company.* During the course of your exit planning and strategy, you will begin to define the direction you want the company to go, which will inform the succession-planning process. You want to pick successors who are going in the same direction.
- *Find the gaps.* As you begin to find out what you need from people on your team in order for them to move into the roles, it might be more helpful to find out what's missing than to

point out what you already have. When you can find the gaps between your talent and what you need, you can begin to develop plans to fill in those gaps or bring in people who can fill in those gaps.

- *Talk to the current team about their goals.* Since your team is a part of the succession planning, even if they don't realize it, you will want to talk to them too. Sit them down and talk to them about what their goals are, what they want to do, and how they want to move forward in the company (or not). By learning their goals and aspirations, you may be able to find a specific plan for them in the succession plan.

- *Point out the obstacles.* Though you want to stay positive during this experience, it's actually more helpful to find the difficulties, as you can address them *now* instead of when they will truly present problems. At this point, think about the obstacles to getting people into the roles you want them in, or obstacles to getting team members the training or experience they need. Problem solving now is a much simpler process.

- *Confer with everyone.* After you have had time to find all the people who will move during the succession plan, talk with all the people on the leadership team and board to see how they feel about the choices you have made. You may have a few conversations about what needs to be done, and you may need to state your case for those who don't get immediate approval.

- *Stay in contact during the process.* Throughout the process of the succession, it is ideal for you to remain active in the conversations. Whenever possible, be a part of the transition by making yourself available for questions and advice. Of course, if the succession happens due to your death, then the person should turn to others who are also aware of the job's responsibilities.

- *Review the plan.* An organization should continue to review the succession plan and update it if team members leave or decide to go in another direction. By being aware of what the succession plan is, it also helps those who are developing other team members.

Succession planning is not the most difficult part of exiting an organization, but it is one of the most important parts. It allows you to know the direction of your company and to be involved in pushing it toward the future.

In addition, this process will help assure your team that your absence is not something they need to fear. Instead, they can look forward to growing their roles and seeing just how valuable they are to the team.

It is important during the exit-planning process to always consider how your decisions will impact on your family. Your family will be directly impacted by the decisions you make during the planning process, the exit, and long after you have exited the business. The next section looks at the family aspects to take into account.

FAMILY MATTERS

It can be incredibly tricky when it comes to exit planning and your family.

Your family is not going anywhere. Even if you exit the business, they will still be around to talk about what you did, how you did it, etc.

According to recent statistics, up to 30 percent of companies will be transferred to a family member at some point in their history. If this is the case, it makes sense to begin to plan for this to happen today.

You can be a part of the conversation about who the next president or CEO will be, and you can make the decision as a family about the timing. In addition, you can create an exit plan that takes into consideration other roles your family members hold, just in case someone decides to leave or someone becomes ill or deceased.

Where this can get tricky is the emotional side of working with your family. You want to help one another, but this may not be the best decision in terms of your business's future. Families are often a part of your business even if they're not in the day-to-day operations.

To remove the emotional aspect of family business, you will want to focus on the facts. To gather the facts, you (and the rest of the family) will want to start thinking about a series of aspects.

- *Consider the family members.* Start with figuring out who is in the company and who is not in the company's activities. While some family members might feel they are the bosses, they may not actually be a part of the leadership structure. To make things as fair and as businesslike as possible, you need to make sure you outline who the actual employees are.
- *Determine the structure of the company.* If you haven't done so already, it's best to create a diagram or a flowchart of all the positions in the company and how they relate to one another. This includes who is in charge of whom and what each position does. If you obtain a greater perspective on how the roles work with one another, you may notice that some positions are redundant.
- *Understand the investment of each family member.* Think carefully about the investment of the family members. You might need to talk to everyone about what they do each day and what they do that might not be a part of their job description. The more facts you can assemble, the better.
- *Learn about their long-term plans (and intentions).* When you talk with the family members, try to get a sense of what they

want to do in the company and where they might want to go next. Some family members may not want to have anything to do with a family business after a while, while others might want to be in ownership positions. The more you know, the more you can set up a transition that will work for everyone. Family members may have moments when things are a bit emotional, and the bonds of your family may be tested. But with a little tact and planning, you can manage these times without long-term damage.

- *Be clear about what you want to do*. Since we are talking about what you want to do and what you want to achieve as a part of your exit from a company, you need to be clear about the fact that you are the one who is deciding what **you want** to do. You're simply finding ways to support this for yourself, and you may not necessarily be looking out for everyone else's wants. In addition, it's best to be as clear as you can about what you are doing. The more mysterious you are, the less support you will get in the process.

- *Be clear about why you are doing what you are doing*. As you will have thought about these decisions for a long time, you will be able to clearly explain why you are doing what you are doing (or why you are doing what you *will* be doing). You need to have these reasons available, as you will be questioned at some point.

- *Be willing to talk*. When family members question you, it's best to sit down and make space for a conversation. In doing so, you can answer questions and attend to any concerns. Again, while you may not change your mind when you talk to your family, the more you are approachable, the more easily you will be able to prevent problems.

- *Be willing to be firm in your decision*. In the end, you need to be clear about what you want and why you want what you want. However, that doesn't mean you need to be mean. Just be clear about what you want and what your decision is. Stick to what you have planned and maintain that consistency. Certainly, there might be hurt feelings, but when your family sees you are making decisions that you want to make, they will eventually come to understand your position.

Families can be challenging, especially when one person thinks he or she should have received something that someone else got. But the more transparent you are during the process, the more effective the process will be, and the more others will buy into what you have decided for yourself.

If you're not sure what you want and what you want to do at this point, you need to start figuring things out. You need to start asking yourself questions, and you need to start identifying the answers that ring true for you. Here are some of the questions you should consider:

- What is best for the company—having it managed by a family member or a manager, or selling the company?
- Will management or ownership or both transfer to family members?
- If ownership is transferred, what would the ownership percentages look like? Will every member get an equal share?
- Do any family members have the skills to take over the business?
- What would the management team look like? Does it have family and/or managers?
- Who will be the family successor, and does he or she need training/development?
- How will the family members fund the purchase of the company, enabling you to retire?
- Do any of the family members have the passion to take the business into the future?

- Which family members will be involved in the business, and what will their roles be?

RESOURCES

Below are some checklists to help you identify your exit readiness and assist with your exit-plan journey.

EXIT-PLANNING PROCESS

Have you completed all the exit-planning components?	% Complete
Retirement Plan	
Financial Plan	
Estate Plan	
Business Plan	
Tax Plan	
Exit Strategy	
Succession Plan	

EXIT READINESS

Exit readiness includes being ready to exit both financially and emotionally. One without the other will cause you to retire without the satisfaction that should go with retirement.

FINANCIAL READINESS

Consider the following questions as they relate to your situation today rather than what you plan to do in the future.	1 = Not Good 5 = Good
Are you certain you have enough money saved for your retirement?	
Do you have sources of income other than your business?	
Do you know exactly how much money you need to maintain your lifestyle when you retire?	

Consider the following questions as they relate to your situation today rather than what you plan to do in the future.	1 = Not Good 5 = Good
Will your lifestyle cost less after you exit your business?	
Is your debt paid off?	
Do you need to receive income from the sale of your business to make your retirement plan work?	
Do you have at least $1 million in investments and savings, other than your business and home?	
Do your retirement funds take into account the impact of inflation and increased health care costs?	
Will your retirement funds be able to cope with increased tax rates during retirement?	
Is your home paid off?	
Is there a big enough buffer in your retirement funds to withstand future economic crises?	
Total	

EMOTIONAL READINESS

Consider the following questions as they relate to your situation today rather than what you plan to do in the future.	1 = Not Good 5 = Good
Is your estate plan up to date?	
Do you have a plan to exit your business?	
Are you ready to exit your business now?	
Do you know exactly what you want to do after you exit your business?	
Do you have something planned for when you exit your business?	
Can the business run effectively without your day-to-day management of the business?	

Consider the following questions as they relate to your situation today rather than what you plan to do in the future.	1 = Not Good 5 = Good
Do you dream about and imagine life after your business?	
Are you able to be less emotionally attached to your business?	
Do you think you have achieved all you wanted to achieve in your business?	
Are you comfortable with change in your life?	
Does the thought of slowing down make you feel comfortable?	
Do you have many interests outside your business?	
Do you find that you are more interested in things outside your business rather than your business?	
Do you want to retire in less than five years?	
Total	

READINESS ASSESSMENT

Financial Readiness	**55**	You have adequate funds to retire, however you are not ready to hand over the keys	You have adequate funds to retire and want to move onto the next adventure after your business
	27	You are neither financially or emotionally ready to exit your business	You are at the point of wanting to move on and need to secure the best price to provide financial security
	0	**35**	**70**
	Emotional Readiness		

41

ASSESSING WHERE YOU ARE

In what level of detail have you considered the following as part of assessing where you are at present?	1 = Not Good 5 = Good
Business	
• Who will take over your responsibilities?	
• What will happen to your employees?	
• Will the company still be in operation?	
• Who legally owns the business?	
• What is the market outlook?	
• Is there a plan for the business?	
• Who will buy your business?	
Financial	
• What is your financial position?	
• How much will you make from the exit?	
• How much money do you need?	
• How much money do you want from the exit?	
• How will the money be distributed?	
Legal	
• What contracts do you have in place?	
• What contracts need to be in place?	
• What legal arrangements are required during the transition?	
• What does your legal team suggest?	
Personal	
• What do you want to do after you exit?	
• What are you going to do in your free time?	
• What happens to your family if the unforeseen happens?	
• What do you need to support your family?	
Tax	
• What taxes do you owe?	
• What taxes will you owe?	
• How can you reduce your taxes?	

In what level of detail have you considered the following as part of assessing where you are at present?	1 = Not Good 5 = Good
Value Creation	
• How can I boost the value of my company?	
• What value creation efforts are already working?	
• What value creation efforts are not working?	

EXIT STRATEGIES

In what level of detail have you considered all the different exit strategy options?	1 = Not Good 5 = Good
Sale to a third party	
Closing of the business/liquidation	
Transfer to a family member	
Sale to management team	
Initial Public Offering (IPO)	

SUCCESSION PLANNING

Have you completed the following steps as part of your succession planning?	% Completed
Determined the skills that are needed in the business?	
Determined the future direction of the company?	
Determined the gaps?	
Determined what the current team's goals and aspirations are?	
Determined what obstacles there might be in moving some staff?	
Conferred with everyone?	

2

GATHER THE RESOURCES YOU NEED

Alone we can do so little, together we can do so much.
—Helen Keller

Though you are a business owner and someone who is invested in the outcome of your company, you can't do everything on your own. You might want to, you may have done everything on your own in the past, and you might not trust anyone else, but you need to let go a little bit now.

When you're planning the future of your company, you need to consider all your options, and getting professionals to help you out is the best way to ensure you have all the facts on hand.

Yes, you will still be a part of this process, but you also need to make sure you're stepping back and letting the pros give you advice about what you need (and what you don't!). As already indicated in the previous chapter, the assistance of lawyers, financial planners, tax professionals, and exit planners familiar with business operations is vital in your exit-planning process. Here we'll dissect the roles each will play in more detail, and we'll discuss how to select the right adviser to work with you. Understanding how all the moving parts work together is vital. First, let's take a broader look at what you need in terms of resources.

WHAT YOU NEED

The best way to plan for anything is to gather information. The more you know, after all, the more you can use the information to your advantage. Though you may not have the information in front of you right now, chances are good that as a business owner, you have the details you need—even if they're in your head right now.

Information is power, as it's been said numerous times.

To make the information gathering more efficient and productive, it can be helpful to:

- *Set aside time outside of business hours.* While you might be able to do some of your information collecting during the business day, it's often best to find time when you are not actively engaged in work (i.e., when you will not be interrupted or distracted). This will ensure you get information that you need and that you will be able to focus on the task at hand.
- *Get help/delegate.* At the same time, you don't need to do everything by yourself. And in the case of larger companies, this may not be possible. Instead, find managers and other trusted staff members who can help you in your data collection efforts. They can collect information about sales, for example, or about the competition.
- *Focus on gathering everything and sorting it later.* Right now, the goal of getting the information you need is to find anything

that seems relevant. Though you may not need it all, the more you can gather, the more you will be able to use—and the more information you will have about your company (in one place!).

- *Realize this will not be an overnight process.* Though it might seem like you needed to gather all this information yesterday, rushing is not the best way to make sure you have the information you need. Instead, you need to focus on how you can get the data that's necessary. Remember, the information you collect is meant to help your company and to secure your future.

In addition, it can be helpful to employ the help of a professional exit planner who can assist you with the coordination of the efforts of the tax, estate, and financial professionals. All these professionals and their roles are discussed in more detail in the next section. They will ask questions and collect data you may not have considered. Some even offer lists of information to help you find what you need to be effective in your strategic planning.

But what are the basics of what you need?

- *You need details about your company.* You need the facts about what your company does, what you expect it to do, etc.
- *You need market information and forecasting.* It's a good idea to collect as many details as possible about what your market is right now and where you expect it to head in the future. You may not be 100 percent sure of these statements or figures, but estimates are helpful.
- *You need a list of the people who work for you, what they do, etc.* You can't make decisions about your company when you don't know who works in it and what they do. Even if you have written the job descriptions yourself, make sure you double

check to see what people *actually* do during their workdays and what this looks like for the company's overall direction.

- *You need current financial statements and previous years' statements.* Numbers are the best kind of information for your exit planning. You need to have the numbers of what you did, what you gained, and what you lost. The financial information is required for both the company and you.
- *You need a list of your goals.* The more you can define what you want, the more you will be able to tailor your exit plan to this dream.

Think about this as an audit of your business and private life to see where it's at so you can get a clear view of what the end game would (and should) look like.

Remember, you don't need to do this alone. You can and should call on professionals to help you.

WHO YOU NEED

Just as when you first hired your team, you need to choose the best people for this job of helping you plan your exit. You need people who can look at what your business does and what it could do, and then they can help you see what the best plan might be.

You need people who can see the bigger picture and people who can help you understand the details. You need people who aren't already involved in the day-to-day activities.

You need someone who understands and isn't caught up in the ownership part of having a business.

EXIT PLANNER

An exit planner can help you from the time you start to figure out how to exit your business to the point of exiting the business. They will help you work through the process of deciding on the why of your plan and what you want to get from the process.

You might look at the exit planner as a partner who will serve as the architect of your success. They will:

- *Listen to your plans.* Just like an architect, the exit planner is someone who will sit with you or talk to you on the phone to see what you want during your exit. They will make sure they understand all your goals, and they will ask questions and write down what they hear. They will also make sure they write up a brief of what you want and ask you to review it before they start creating a plan.

- *Let you know what parts are available*. With your ideas in mind, the exit planner will then let you know what parts are available for you to use in building your plan (i.e., retirement planning, business planning, etc.). When you have this information, you can ask questions, make decisions, or decide on a new strategy based on what you have learned.

- *Give advice about what works/doesn't work*. The exit planner will give you a sense of how these parts might fit together, which ones will work, which ones will not, etc. Based on what they know of you, they might offer you a certain strategy, or they might continue to ask questions until they feel they are in complete understanding.

- *Show you who will do the heavy lifting*. At the same time, the exit planner is not someone who will necessarily manage your tax needs or your legal needs. They will point out whom you need to hire, but the exit planner is mainly your strategist, your architect, the one who shows you the way.

With their help, you will be able to manage your:

- retirement planning
- financial planning
- estate planning
- business planning
- tax planning
- exit strategy
- succession planning
- and more

They can also help you when you're unsure about how to approach certain situations while also helping you better understand what needs to be done next.

You might employ someone like this to make sure you stay on track with your goals for planning. Since there are a lot of steps to take, it can be the person who prods you along. They might spend time with you on helping you refine and adjust your goals before you take any actual action. Though this might not seem like a lot of fun or like it's getting you anywhere, the more time you invest in a good plan, the better the overall strategy will work.

The exit planner ensures all the necessary parts are aligned and that other advisers take all aspects into account. They also ensure that all the other professionals on the team stay aligned with the overall plan and with one another.

Think of this person as the architect of the building of your financial future. It is someone who is not only the person who gives you the information you need and helps you set up the strategy that you want but also the person who is going to work to ensure all the necessary parts are in place.

It cannot be stressed enough that the exit planner is the architect of your success. Exit planners can't take the steps for you, but they can help you set up a plan so you can follow through. They can take all your ideas and put them into a step-by-step plan to follow.

The earlier you can meet with this person, the more you can prepare for the future. The future will be here more quickly than you might anticipate, so planning now is the best way to prevent surprises down the road.

FINANCIAL PLANNER

Money may not be everything, but it's certainly a big part of exit planning. You need to know you have enough money available for the next stage of your life. You need to make sure that all the pieces are in place to give you the things you need to have when the time comes for you to not be at work anymore.

While you might understand the basics of budgeting and you know that setting aside money is a good thing, this is only part of what you need to know—and this is why you need to have a professional who can give you the extra information to help you set things up right the first time (and possibly the only time).

A financial planner will help you understand how to plan for retirement, how to manage your investments, and how to set up your finances for the future.

When it comes to investing in your future, you need to come up with a plan of attack in terms of investing. Many people never feel ready for this type of financial strategy, but it's also the most consistently effective way to plan for the future—no matter when you are starting to plan.

The more you can invest, the more likely you are to make a return on that investment. Consider this: stocks and other related investments have shown that over the course of their lifetimes, they continue to show gains. This is even the case in the recovery period after the 2008 economic downturn.

In addition, financial planners can help you with other financial support systems, such as life insurance. Plus, there are disability, trauma, and income protection insurance plans for unforeseen events other than death, where the person is not able to work either for a period of time (e.g., heart attack) or permanently (e.g., stroke or accident).

Because you may want to have an added layer of security in a situation where you might die before you retire, the financial planner can help you choose the insurance portfolio that is best for you.

Financial planners can also help with assessing where you are right now in terms of your investments and savings and where you want to and need to be. They can talk you through the different levels of risk, and they can help you better understand whether you need to take more of a risk or if you should do something that is safer.

They can also help establish financial systems for your business and your family, ensuring your transition out of the company is smooth.

Not all financial planners will provide all these types of services, but it is worth looking into if you have a history of not being able to handle your money effectively. You can also sit down with this planner and your family to decide what sort of financial future they should have and what the strategies might be to support this goal.

The more involved everyone is at this stage, the more everyone will understand if other financial changes need to happen in order to support your long-term goals.

LAWYER

When you're starting to think about exiting your company, you need all the help you can get—no matter how smart you are and no matter how experienced you are. An attorney can be an invaluable resource in this process and can support the strategy of your exit planner, helping to ensure documents are filed correctly and legal steps are taken when they need to be taken.

The list of ways in which a lawyer can help you in your exit planning includes:

- *Company sales.* When you're looking to sell your company, you need to have a legal team to ensure everyone on each side of the table is getting what they want and what they expect. You need to make sure the contract(s) you sign are inclusive of your needs and goals while also including protective elements, if needed.
- *Ownership changes.* With any changes in ownership or management, it can help to have legal counsel alongside you. Lawyers are essential when you are selling your company to another owner. Even though the other person might be a family member, you still want to have a professional there to write up the new ownership documents and to review any documents from the buyer's legal team.
- *Contract reviews.* Though you may not need to have a lawyer present during all your exit planning, you will want to have one on board for when you need to rewrite contracts or review old contracts. Even with contracts you have drawn up in the past, you still want to have someone to review them, and an attorney is the best person for the job.
- *Taxes.* While not all lawyers are certified or knowledgeable about tax law, they can offer support when it comes to handling business taxes and tax issues. The more legal support you have, the more you can focus on taking action in the best way possible (or you will have support if you need to argue against a tax issue).
- *Estate planning.* You will also need a lawyer to draw up a will for you. This can outline what you want to happen to the company when you're not the one in charge or should you die before retiring. In addition, an attorney can help you with managing the properties you own and ensuring that there are

clear agreements as to who gets what when the time comes for ownership to change (either purposely or suddenly).

- *Business advice.* At the very least, using a lawyer is a great idea when you have questions about your exit strategy. They can talk with you about what you may need to remember and what else you might need to do. An attorney can also give you business advice, which can come in handy when you have long-term plans in place.

The more legal support and advice you have, the more prepared you will be for anything that might come up during your exit-planning process. You can't know everything, and while legal support might seem expensive, it can also be the best investment you make in your company's future and in your future.

TAX PROFESSIONAL

No matter what kind of business you are in, you need to deal with taxes. The more advice you can get on what the taxes might be, what you might expect to pay, and how you might be able to diminish your tax bill(s), the better.

Since tax codes are always changing, you need to have someone to help you navigate their complexity and apply the rules appropriately.

Some of the ways in which a tax professional can help include:

- business purchase and sales price allocations
- partial business transitions
- risk management techniques
- buy/sell agreements

True, this list looks similar to what other professionals can do for you during the exit-planning process, but a tax professional will focus on the tax ramifications.

A tax professional looks at the way(s) in which all these actions might impact your tax situation. This might include how much you need to pay in taxes, how high your tax rate might be, etc. In looking at each of your exit-planning steps and seeing what you will be facing, a tax professional can help you understand what the risks are and what the benefits might be of choosing certain actions.

Though the tax professional can analyze your activities and assess the outcomes in terms of your taxes, they may not be able to do this in relation to the larger exit plan. Thus, it's best for the tax professional to work in conjunction with the exit planner. You can take the plan you have and then show it to the tax professional.

In addition, it's a good idea for you to sit down with the tax professional before, during, and after each major financial transaction you make. In doing so, you will be able to see the outcomes and assess what might need to happen next in order to prepare.

For many, tax support is about understanding the possible tax payments in the future and minimizing the tax bill. When you know this information, you can set aside the money now for future payments. This can prepare you for these payments and ensure the rest of your financial plans aren't impacted significantly.

BUSINESS BROKER

If you plan on selling your business, you will want to have the services of a business broker. This is a professional who understands the process of selling a company, what steps to take, and how to get the most for the client. After all, you want to get the most out of your business sale. Finding the right business broker when selling a business may help you receive the best possible price. If you don't have the time or experience to negotiate the business sale privately, then a business broker is the right choice for you. Business brokers are experts at selling businesses; it is what they do every day. Similar to real estate agents, accountants, and lawyers, they provide a service, which is to help you sell your business. Business broker commissions range from 7 percent to 10 percent of the final selling price for the business.

The relationship with a business broker can look like this:

- *You share your exit plan goals.* While this may not be necessary, it can help to contextualize the reason for your desire to sell your company. This might also help the broker see how you are motivated to sell, and that can be a part of the negotiation process.
- *You hand over information about your company.* In order to get the most for your company, the broker will need to have all the information you have about your company. This will help them value your company, assess its worth in relation to the market, and better understand how to broker a deal with an investor or other company. Business brokers are well placed to value your business when you start your exit-planning process, and most brokers provide this service on a fee basis. Valuations are discussed in more detail in the next chapter.
- *You assess the offers you have received for your company.* The broker will collect offers from other companies/investors interested in purchasing your company. These offers will be collected based on what you have said your sales parameters are, including the minimum or desired price. When you have these offers, you can look at them to see if any are interesting to you or if you need to continue to look for new offers.

- *You negotiate with the buyers.* In some cases, you might be interested in negotiating with the prospective buyers. You might offer certain terms to the investor, or you might listen to the terms the investor wants to share with you. In either case, you will have an opportunity to see what else you can get until you both agree to the sale, or one of you decides you don't want to broker the deal together. Again, during this process, the business broker is handling the transactions with your best interests in mind.
- *You finalize the sale.* When you agree with the buyer to the terms of the sale, the broker (and your attorney, hopefully) will work on finalizing the terms and getting everything in writing so the agreement is clear. You will then get a check on the determined date, pay a broker fee, and start your new life.

While this process has been simplified to make it more understandable, the process of brokering a sale can be complex, problematic, and emotional.

This is why it's crucial you have a professional in your corner, someone who can help you get the deal that you deserve and not just any sale.

YOUR FAMILY

As we discussed while exploring family and the intricacies of succession, it bears repeating here that family-owned businesses involve more than just the primary owner and operator. As you muster the allies you'll need to formulate and execute a successful exit plan, it's vital to keep family stakeholders in mind as pivotal in your overall effort.

In the case of a family-run and owned business, you need to bring your family into the discussions about what might happen next when you are gone.

At the same time, these discussions might bring up long-term planning for the entire family. You might begin a conversation that allows for the next ten to twenty years to be covered and organized in terms of exits.

The more you plan now, the less you have to plan later. (And you'll be more stable in your family business.)

- *Know what they want.* While it's been said before, it bears repeating: find out what your family wants from the business and its future. The more you can clarify everyone's actual goals, the more you will be able to come up with an agreeable plan for your exit. Instead of assuming someone is going to take over, for example, find out from that person whether that is his or her goal.
- *Get opinions.* You're going to hear opinions from your family, so you may as well ask for them. Find out what everyone thinks about your exit and how you might approach it. They may have information you haven't considered yet.
- *Write out your agreements.* When you have figured out what you want to do in relation to your family and your exit plan, write out what you have agreed to. This will help to solidify the terms of your agreements, and it will ensure there is a record of your conversations and what you said you would do in the future.
- *Get a legal team involved.* To further make those conversations effective and productive, make sure to call in an attorney to help you with creating legal documents about agreements and promises within the family unit. In doing so, everyone has a chance to see what will happen if someone doesn't follow through on the agreements, and they can spend a little more time thinking about whether they are as certain as they thought they were.

- *Be open to changes.* Even though it seems counterproductive to be open to changes after finally getting to an agreement, families do have a little more say-so in what happens in a family-run business. At the same time, make sure the adjustments you make are based on thorough research, analysis, and more conversations with the same people who put the original agreements into place.
- *Use their expertise.* Some of your family members might have knowledge and expertise about the company that you don't have or don't remember. Be sure to tap into that information, since it may be something that a legal or tax professional may not consider.
- *Know your limits.* In the end, family might be the most important thing to you, but when they're simply arguing because they don't want to see you go, you need to stop the conversations that don't end. After all, this is your decision to exit, and you can do as you please. When you remind them that you're just trying to do what's best for everyone, you can start setting limits and avoid conversations that don't seem to end with any agreements.

Family is forever, and you may never get everyone to agree on everything all the time. But with a little patience, you might be able to make a clean transition—and still be able to sit at the table during holidays without having awkward silences.

HOW YOU SELECT A TEAM OF COMPETENT PROFESSIONALS

It is extremely important that you assemble a competent team that includes an exit planner, a financial planner, and legal, tax, and business broker professionals. When you are planning an exit, this might be the best investment you make, and it should not be seen as an added expense.

You will find a list of questions that follow to help you assess who will work best for you on your exit journey. Obviously, the right answers to most of these questions depend on your individual situation and needs. These questions will help you select the right professional when the time comes. Do not be afraid to shop around or to change your adviser if you are not comfortable

After your interviews, you'll want to perform a quick background check. Contact your state's or country's board where the adviser is registered to check the status of his or her license, or to find out if any disciplinary action has been taken against him or her.

EXIT PLANNER

If you choose the right exit planner for your business, it will pave the way to an easier business transition down the track. Look for these four attributes in an exit-planning adviser:

1. Understands that he or she does not possess all the skills necessary to create a comprehensive exit plan
2. Has knowledge of and training in a proven exit-planning system
3. Has worked for years with numerous business owners
4. Creates written plans that cover all aspects of exit planning and includes specific action items assigned to various advisers, with stated due dates

Here are some questions that you should ask a potential exit planner:

1. *What are your qualifications?*
   Ask what qualifications the person has obtained to call him or herself an exit planner and how long he or she has been preparing exit plans.

2. *What kind of clients do you see, and what services do you provide? Do you have any specialties?*

   Does he or she have clients like you and experience with businesses similar to yours? You want to make sure your exit planner understands your type of business. Go with someone whose offerings suit your needs.

3. *What do you mean by "exit planning"?*

   You want the answer to be all about you and your goals.

4. *What do you do when you create an exit plan? Where do you start?*

   He or she should say something about your goals and the need to figure out how much money you need to live the way you want to after you leave your business. Ideally, you want the adviser to talk about:

   - Money: how much will you need from the sale of your business to achieve financial independence?
   - Time: how many more years do you need to stay in the business to reach that value?
   - Successor: can the successor you envision pay you that value or should you consider other buyers?

5. *What do you include in your exit plans? Can you show me an example of a plan you have created?*

   An adviser should talk about how your goals drive the plan. He or she should make recommendations with specific action items, while assigning due dates and responsibilities.

   There is no one set structure for an exit plan, which means there is wide variation. Ask to see a sample exit plan. Even better, ask to see an actual plan the adviser has created for a client (with all the identifying information removed). Advisors who do exit planning will gladly supply one of these. You are looking to see if this adviser has an inclusive process, not necessarily the details of the plan.

6. *Are you able to assist in finding out what my business is worth?*
   Any exit plan starts with this important piece of information. Make sure your exit planner has the ability to assess or engage other professionals to determine the value of your business.

7. *Assuming that my business is not worth enough today to support the lifestyle I want when I exit, what will you do for me?*
   Don't expect detailed answers at this point. Expect to hear something about growing business value, reducing taxes, and minimizing business risk.

8. *Who will be involved in this plan?*
   An exit planner shouldn't be the sole person developing your exit plan with you, as he or she is not an expert in all fields. However, the exit planner should be experienced enough to coordinate a team of advisers who have the expertise.

9. *Who will look after my business most of the time? Who will be doing the work?*
   Some companies have a team approach rather than an individual approach. It really depends on what your preference is. You need to be comfortable with the person actually providing the advice, so make sure you're not going to be shunted over to a more junior person when you need to talk to someone.

10. *How do you work alongside my other business advisers?*
    Most business owners have a collection of advisers, each with his or her own specialty and agenda. Your exit planner should be charged with integrating all the advice from all the advisors into one comprehensive exit plan.

11. *Once you create my plan, what will we do if circumstances change?*
    Sometimes businesses don't perform to the owner's expectations or the child an owner thought would succeed is no longer interested, or the key employee earmarked for succession leaves the company. A good exit planner creates an exit plan that is flexible enough to adapt to these and other changes.

12. *If I decide to transfer my company to my key employees (or child), and I know they don't have any money, what ideas do you have to handle that?*
    The adviser should describe strategies used to get you your entire purchase price before you relinquish any control of the company.

13. *I want to sell to a third party. What do buyers look for? Can you help me improve my business to make it attractive to owners?*
    Regardless of industry, there are several characteristics buyers look for in acquisitions. See the ten value factors in chapter 3.

14. *What happens to my company and family if I don't live to see my exit date?*
    A good exit planner will put mechanisms in place to protect your business and your family should you die or become disabled before executing your planned exit.

15. *How do you invoice for your services? Is it done monthly, biannually?*

Find out exactly how your exit planner will bill. Is it by the hour, or is it for the value that he or she provides? Look for an exit planner who bills on a fixed fee, project basis rather than on an hourly basis. Ask how often you will expect to receive an invoice.

16. *What sort of access will I be given to the data you hold about my business?*

Make sure that you will be given full access to all your business data. Exit planners can provide you with information to update your business, estate, or succession plans.

17. *Can you provide business advice and assist in the financial management of my business?*

Consider an exit planner that will provide regular reports on your business with additional commentary.

18. *Are you available year-round?*

When you're running a small business, you're going to need help all year, so make sure that your exit planner can be there whenever you have important information to divulge or request. It's important that you understand how often he or she will be in touch and that you're comfortable with this. Will there be regular monthly meetings and reports?

19. *How much contact do you have with your clients?*

Some exit planners hold an initial planning meeting, and then you see them only every so often, and that's all you get. Others might have monthly meetings to monitor the progress. It really depends on how much support you think you may need and how much communication is necessary between these visits.

20. *Do you have testimonials?*
    Any professional, experienced exit planner should have testimonials and references you should be able to call. Ask to talk to a current client to see if he or she is happy with the service provided.

Finally, there's one last question you want to ask of yourself after meeting with a potential exit planner:

21. *Did he or she ask me questions and seem to be interested in me?*
    Exit planning is all about finding out as much information as possible about the business owner and the business. The exit planner should ask you questions and provide a guide on the length of time the exit plan will take to develop. However, the period of time may not be confirmed until after seeing your business in action, including meeting staff, looking at systems and plans, and evaluating the capacity for sale.

FINANCIAL PLANNER

The challenge in financial advice concerns conflict of interests. Your concern is to make the best decisions for yourself and your family so that your retirement savings grow, you have appropriate insurance, and you are creating security. However, your interests may not coincide with those of a financial planner who may be rewarded for you taking out a certain type of insurance.

Large consultancies have considerable depth of expertise, but many entrepreneurs and small-business owners may find that a large firm that specializes in this area, or someone attached to a broader professional service practice or corporate banking division, is a better fit. This is because a wider understanding of the issues owner-managed businesses face is important to getting this advice right.

To help find a suitable financial planner, get recommendations from business owners whose financial needs, outlook, or stage of life is similar to yours. Before contacting planners, look them up online and on LinkedIn to get a sense of what each firm is like. Many experts say that a fee-only adviser is preferable, to eliminate conflicts of interest and ensure they always act with your best interest at heart.

Once you have short-listed potential advisers, take one more step before setting up appointments to meet: find out whether each has ever been disciplined for any unlawful or unethical behavior.

When you have your initial interview, here are some questions you should ask:

1. *What licenses, credentials, or other certifications do you have?*
   If you want someone to manage your money, then look for a registered financial adviser.

2. *What services do you/does your firm provide?*
   Some planners are just investment advisers and only provide you advice on your investments. Other planners do comprehensive financial planning around retirement, insurance, estate planning, and tax planning. Find someone whose offerings suit your needs.

3. *How do you charge for your services, and how much?*
   If you didn't see this information on the planner's website, ask whether there's an initial planning fee, whether the planner charges a percentage for assets under management, and whether the planner makes money from selling you a specific

product. Not only should you know how much the service will cost you but it can help you determine whether the planner has an incentive to sell you things.

4. *What types of clients do you specialize in?*
Some financial advisers have a niche, so find out what this niche is and see if it corresponds with your needs.

5. *Could I see a sample financial plan?*
There is no one set structure for a financial plan, which means there is wide variation. Ask for a sample so that you can see if it is an in-depth analysis with lots of charts and graphs or a simple plan of a financial situation. Make sure the sample provided suits your preferred format.

6. *What is your investment approach?*
If you have a strong preference for a particular financial investment philosophy, ask the adviser what his or her philosophy is. For example, if you prefer to use low-cost funds, you can ask whether he or she plans to use actively managed funds or passive investments.

7. *How much contact do you have with your clients?*
Some planners hold an initial planning meeting and then you see him or her once a year, and that's it. Others might have quarterly check-ins. If you are looking for more support, then you need to convey this to the adviser. Of course, you will probably pay more for this added service.

8. *Will I be working only with you or with a team?*
This question will also help you see how often you'll be in touch with your adviser. Some may only meet once a year with limited contact throughout the year. Some companies have a

team approach rather than an individual approach. It really depends on what your preference is.

9. *What makes your client experience unique?*
   This will give you insight into whether the adviser's strengths are the ones you seek in a planner.

Finally, there's one last question you want to ask yourself after meeting with a potential planner:

10. *Did he or she ask me questions and seem to be interested in me?*
    Financial planning is about looking at the person's individual circumstance rather than just numbers. It should be based on your goals, financial background, beliefs about money, etc. So the adviser should spend time getting to know you and your business.

LAWYER

When you hire a lawyer, he or she will be handling some of your business's most sensitive legal issues, so it's important to hire someone you feel comfortable working with and can trust.

Lawyers will often provide a free or very low-cost consultation to discuss the details of your situation and give you an opportunity to ask some basic questions. This meeting should help you decide whether you should proceed with a particular lawyer. Generally speaking, you'll want to have a list of questions in mind to ask during the meeting. You should feel comfortable enough asking questions that relate to the lawyer's expertise, experience, fees, special knowledge, and management of your work.

You can go into a more detailed discussion of your needs and ask more specific questions along the way.

Here are some key questions to help you find a lawyer who is just the right fit for your business:

1. *What are your qualifications and how much experience do you have within my industry?*
   Find out if the lawyers you're screening have worked with a company similar to yours and if you can speak with any previous clients. Experience in the special needs of your business is important to get the best results.

2. *What is your approach to conflict resolution?*
   Find out how much of a lawyer's time is spent battling it out in court and how much is devoted to mediating disputes. Then decide which approach you're more comfortable with.

3. *Who will look after my business most of the time? How many partners are there? Will there be anyone else handling my work?*
   Most lawyers assign work to paralegals. Take caution against lawyers who delegate an extensive amount of work. Taking the time to explain something to your lawyer and then having it reexplained to a paralegal could cost you more money and might alter the message. While some work can certainly be delegated, be sure that you understand who will be handling which tasks. Consider choosing a practice comparable in size to your business. Sometimes smaller practices suit smaller businesses.

4. *What kind of clients do you see most often?*
   If the lawyer already has clients in your industry, it means he or she will have more knowledge of how to best deal with your needs.

5. *Do you have any clients who could create conflicts?*

   Find out if your prospective lawyer is working for other clients, such as competitors or former business partners, who could pose a conflict of interest. If so, problems could arise, and you may not feel comfortable sharing competitive information with the lawyer.

6. *What is your communication style? How long do you typically take to get back to people?*

   Some lawyers prefer to correspond primarily via e-mail or phone; others don't communicate much beyond scheduled office meetings. If you want someone who is available to answer your questions as they come up, be sure to find out what their communication style is and whether it works for you.

7. *How do you invoice for your services?*

   Find out exactly how they bill so there are no surprises. Some may bill for minimum increments of ten minutes, while others might not bill for less than an hour. Also, ask about other expenses, such as research and paralegal fees.

   If the lawyer will not send you clear information about how he or she bills for the services, beware, as you could be in for some big surprises about what things cost down the track.

   Look for a lawyer who bills on a fixed fee, project basis rather than on an hourly basis (unless you are engaging in litigation when court rules often dictate hourly rate charging). The lawyer you choose should promise to never send you an unexpected bill for quick phone calls or e-mails.

8. *Are there ways to reduce the cost of your services?*
   Don't be discouraged by what seem to be high fees. Ask if there are ways to cut down on costs. For example, you might be able to save money by rounding up documents yourself.

9. *Do you belong to any specialized bar associations?*
   You want a lawyer who keeps up with the latest legal and business matters. Be sure to ask whether he or she belongs to such groups as the local bar association, chamber of commerce, or a small-business advisory board.

10. *Do you make referrals to other lawyers?*
    You should be able to consult your lawyer on all sorts of legal or financial issues, knowing he or she will be willing to put you in touch with his or her colleagues on a specialized issue he or she lacks experience in. Lawyers must have specialized training in one or more specific practice areas, such as business, intellectual property, or corporate law. They are not experts in all matters. Don't use a lawyer that is wary of referring you to another lawyer.

TAX PROFESSIONAL

Business owners of all types can benefit from hiring a tax professional. However, it is important to get the best one for your needs. An accountant might be great at what he or she does—but not the right fit for your business. Good tax professionals do more than just figure the numbers; they communicate what the numbers mean.

Like most people, you're probably not sure how to choose a tax professional. Referrals are a good place to start. Shop around, interview accountants, and figure out which one is the best fit for you and your business. Hopefully you will find a professional who can take your business to the next level and help you avoid costly mistakes.

Before you spend your hard-earned cash, here are some simple questions you can ask to protect yourself and find the right professional for your situation.

1. *What are your qualifications? Do you have experience with taxes?*
   There are many types of tax accountants out there, so it's good to find out who you're working with so you're sure your business affairs are handled correctly. Make sure they have the credentials to back up their claim as an accountant, as some aren't technically accountants.

   It's good to choose a tax professional that is part of an association. The two main associations are Chartered Accountants and CPA.

2. *How long has the practice been operating, and how long have you been with the practice?*
   Find out how long they have been preparing returns, providing advice, and whether they usually work with clients whose financial situations are similar to your own.

3. *What kind of clients do you see, and what services do you provide?*
   Do they have clients like you and experience in the services you need? You want to make sure your tax professional understands your type of business. For example, a restaurant will have certain rules to follow for wages and tips, just as a construction business must deal with issues related to contract workers, and a real estate development firm will have certain criteria about how income is reported. You need a tax professional who has worked with other businesses like yours and knows the ins and outs of the industry. Ask to talk to a current client to see if he or she is happy with the service provided.

4. *What other services do you provide? Do you have expertise in areas relevant to me?*
   If you want a tax professional to help you grow your business before exiting, you will need expertise in estate planning, business planning, strategic planning, budgeting, and cash flow management. You need to make sure their experience and skill set match the service that you're after.

   Are you looking for business advice or a tax professional that just pumps out tax returns?

   As well as tax reporting, the best tax advisers will be proactive in helping you organize your affairs, maintain a good working knowledge of your business, and act as a sounding board for long-term aspirations. They should provide a perspective between your personal position and business affairs.

5. *Will you represent me if I am audited?*
   A tax professional should stand by his or her tax return and represent you in the unlikely case you are audited (for an additional fee). Don't take on one that is reluctant to assist.

6. *How do you keep track of changes in a client's circumstances?*
   Services should include checkups on how any plans are going.

7. *Who will look after my business most of the time? Who will be doing the work? What is the size of the practice?*
   Tax professionals will often outsource work to a third party. This doesn't mean their services are bad, but you want to be sure they are forthright about who is doing the work. If you want to talk with someone familiar with your bookkeeping, and that's a third party, it likely will be difficult to speak with them directly.

8. *Are you a conservative or more aggressive tax professional?*
Some tax professionals want to write off everything they possibly can, while others take a more conservative approach. It's important to figure out where you fall on the spectrum and find a professional who agrees with your philosophy. If your tax professional tells you they specialize in finding red flags that could trigger audits, they may be hesitant to maximize your deductions.

9. *How do you handle working with multiple entities?*
If you have more than one entity under your name, be sure the professional you hire can manage them simultaneously, as not all tax professionals possess this skill. If you own rental property and a retail store, for example, you'll need a tax professional who can coordinate and track money moving between those entities.

10. *How will your practice help me develop my business?*
Consider choosing a practice that will partner with you in the development of your business to help obtain the best value at the time of sale.

11. *What sort of access will I be given to the data you hold about my business?*
Make sure you will be given full access to all your business data. Tax professionals can provide you with information to update your business plan or a tender document.

12. *Can you provide business advice and assist in the financial management of my business?*
Consider practices that will provide regular financial reports on your business with additional commentary.

13. *Will you return my calls within a reasonable time? How long will you take to complete your work?*

    Clear processes should be established to keep you well informed. How quickly can you expect to hear back from your tax professional? Make sure you have a clear understanding of how and how quickly your accountant will return your call or e-mail.

    "Turnaround time" is often a common complaint from small businesses regarding their existing accountants. If your tax professional takes three months to finish your work, maybe it's time that you moved on.

14. *Are you available year-round?*

    Some tax firms shut their doors at the end of the tax year and only reopen for the following tax season. But when you're running a small business, you're going to need help all year-round. The tax professional should get to learn about your business and your life. It's important that you understand how often they'll be in touch and that you're comfortable with this.

15. *Are you familiar with the accounting/software package I use in my business? What technology do you use?*

    Establish how information will be accessed and shared. You shouldn't choose a tax professional based on the tax program he or she uses, but it's a good question to ask. Xero is commonly used for small businesses, which means your information would likely be easily transferred between different tax professionals. Hiring a professional who uses more obscure tax software won't affect the quality of the work, but it might make it tricky to switch tax professionals.

The adoption of cloud accounting software is saving businesses thousands of dollars, and hours of bookwork every week. Ask if the firm works with cloud accounting software.

16. *How will you communicate with me? How will I be informed, particularly of any changes to legislation?*
It's important to know how you'll be communicating with your accountant on a regular basis. Do they use technology such as Skype, GoToMeeting, Lync, or others to enhance web meetings to describe concepts and run scenarios?

Every tax professional is different when it comes to frequency of communication for tax planning purposes. Ask about a prospective tax professional's approach and be sure you're satisfied with the degree of communication.

17. *How do you bill for your services, and what will I get for my money?*
Be sure to get a good understanding of the charges and how they work. It avoids unwanted surprises, and you have clarity before moving forward.

Some questions within this section are:

- *What does the project or subscription include?*
- *Do they price each job before they start, so you can both agree to the scope and terms?*
- *Do they allow you to pay by the month to spread the burden on cash flow?*
- *Do they charge for each phone call or e-mail, or are these questions included?*

- *Do they charge by the hour (and are therefore potentially rewarded for being inefficient), or do they charge for the value that they provide?*

Regardless of the billing approach, be sure to get an estimate of a tax professional's likely fees. Provide a copy of your previous year's tax returns so they can familiarize themselves with your business before giving a quote.

18. *What can you do to keep the fees down?*
    The better organized you are, the less time your tax professional will need to search for information, which translates to lower fees. Send a spreadsheet or accountancy program file that contains all your income and expenses rather than all your invoices; give list of charities vs. copies of all letters/cancelled checks. Provide most of the data at one time and not in pieces, because the more your tax professional has to pick up and put down a file, the greater the cost.

19. *Will you review my past tax returns at no charge?*
    An outstanding tax adviser should because it shouldn't take too long. A capable professional should ask you to send relevant paperwork in advance of your meeting so you can spend your meeting time more productively.

20. *Do I need a tax lawyer?*
    Tax lawyers are those professionals who have chosen to specialize in tax law. They often have a master of laws degree in taxation in addition to the required degree. Lawyers are best at complex legal matters, such as preparing estate tax returns.

BUSINESS BROKER

Choosing to sell your business is a big decision that brings with it a variety of challenges. Some sellers make huge mistakes by deciding to sell their business on their own. They do not invest adequate strategic resources, thought, or planning into preparing their business for sale, which costs them real money. This is usually due to most of their time being spent on running the business, responding to customers, etc.

They also make a huge mistake in not choosing the right business broker to handle the sale of their business. Like any industry, there are good and bad business brokers. You need to make sure you are choosing the right business broker with adequate experience to handle the sale of your business, in order to maximize its sale value.

It's helpful to have a professional business broker help you with the business selling process and lead you to the best possible outcome. You only get one chance to sell your business, so make sure you ask these questions of your potential business broker:

1. *How many years have you been selling businesses?*
    It is imperative to hire a business broker or business brokerage firm that has years of experience in selling businesses. You should ask the agent how long he or she has been with the firm. That will provide you with further insight regarding the agent's experience level.

2. *How many brokerage offices do you have or are you affiliated with? Do you cobroker?*
    The more brokerage offices or affiliates, the better outcome for the sale of your business. Cobrokerage is an advantage for the seller because the broker utilizes their network to sell the business. This increases the probability of selling in less than the average selling time.

3. *How many businesses have you sold in your career in relation to the number of years you have been working as a broker?*

   Remember, a business broker is a salesman, so find out how many sales have been accomplished during his/her years of experience. The more businesses they have sold, the more experience they will have at putting deals together.

4. *How many businesses do you sell a year?*

   The average business broker will sell eight to ten businesses a year. If they only sell one or two, is it because they sell larger businesses or is it because they are not motivated to sell more or not good enough at selling more businesses per year? The answer will be important in making your decision.

5. *How long does an average sale take?*

   Time kills deals. Make sure the business broker you select is responsive in getting things accomplished and moving things along. Deals tend to deteriorate when parties aren't moving forward on a deal at all times.

   Businesses on average typically take six to nine months to sell but might extend to twelve months for some types of businesses. Your broker should be able to tell you his or her average. However, keep in mind that the seller has a significant influence on the selling duration by setting a reasonable asking price and contract terms.

6. *What industries have you sold businesses in?*

   Business brokers will often have a type of specialized business that they are best at selling due to several factors, such as location, experience, and personal preferences. It is highly advisable to choose a business broker who has sold a few businesses similar to yours in the past twelve months. These sold businesses should be comparable sales in price, business type, and size.

7. *How many listings do you have?*

The average business broker will have fifteen to twenty listings at any given time. If they have less than the average, it might be important to know why they have fewer listing than other brokers. Is it because they are not motivated to obtain more listings? Are they new and that is why they don't have more listings? Is it because they are not good at obtaining listings? Or are they good at selling their listings, and that is why they have fewer listings?

8. *Do you have a database of buyers? If so, how many?*

Business brokerage is a network, connection, and word-of-mouth sort of business. You should hire a business brokerage firm that has a database of buyers. Professional, experienced business brokers will run a query of all their buyers in their buyer databases that could be a good fit for your business. Ask if they have a list of clients who have missed out on recent sales; they might already have a few clients in their database to whom they can suggest your business.

9. *Do you have testimonials?*

Any professional, experienced business broker should have testimonials and references from a variety of sources, not just past clients, that you should be able to call. However, business sales are confidential, and a business broker cannot disclose the information on any sold businesses without the seller's permission.

10. *What can I expect in regards to the level of communication from you?*

Direct, open, and constant communication with your business broker about expectations and other issues is critical in selling your business. Make sure you let your business broker know what your expectations are for letting you know how things are progressing (e.g., once-a-week updates, call only when something is going on, etc.). It is important that sellers and business brokers have at least weekly dialogues to see how things are moving forward. Find out how many buyers have responded and any feedback on all buyers who have expressed an interest in your business for sale. Returning phone calls in a timely manner is critical. Make sure the business broker you select is good about getting back promptly to potential buyers.

11. *What does the listing agreement/contract include? What is your service charge? Is it negotiable?*

You don't want to hire a business broker who simply claims he/she can get the best price for you. A good broker should be able to get you not only the best possible price but also the best terms for your business. At a minimum, a broker should be able to justify his/her fee by getting you more than if you tried to sell the business on your own.

The listing agreement/contract should include: length of time they will be representing you (three to twelve months is typical); how they are going to advertise and market your business for sale (get the details and budget); how often they should be contacting you about buyers and deal updates (at least weekly); what happens when the agreement expires (with all the buyers who have signed confidentiality agreements during this period, what happens if you find a buyer); what is the commission when the agreement expires, will they cooperate with other business brokers/agents on your listing (this opens the market to more buyers), etc. Get everything in writing so you both know what the expectations are.

Have the business broker determine the valuation of your business before you sign a listing agreement. This is very important since over 70 percent of all small businesses never sell, usually due to the price being too high for the marketplace or unrealistic terms and conditions on selling the business. There are many ways to structure a deal—you need a business broker who can be honest with you and discuss these variances with you.

Business brokers are compensated by the seller with a commission fee arrangement based on the sale price. Commission, or success fee, is paid only upon a successful sale of a business. Brokers tend to charge 8–10 percent commissions of a business sale plus any additional fee for marketing expense. Sometimes a minimum flat fee applies instead of fixed-percentage commission. For example, a commission agreement might involve a flat amount of typically $10,000 instead of a fixed percentage for businesses that are sold at $100,000 or less. For such a small business, the minimum flat fee actually works out to be a higher percentage than the 8–10 percent industry typical commission. All business brokers are required by law to advise the client that commission is negotiable, therefore giving you the right to discuss the commission structure.

12. *What is your success rate (closing ratio) in the last twelve months?*
Success rate is the number of sales successfully closed (sold) compared to total listed businesses with the business broker in a specific time period. Ask for the rate for the last twelve

months. Obviously, the higher the percentage, the better. Business brokers stay in the business by knowing how to keep a constant flow of business sales into a successful conclusion (i.e., consistently getting deals to the closing table).

13. *How do you evaluate what my business is worth? What resources will you utilize to evaluate my business?*
A professional, experienced business broker will evaluate your business based upon a thorough review and receipt of key business information from you. Experienced business brokers will not take the listing if the seller's expectations are not in line with the broker's evaluation.

14. *What is your estimation of selling price? How did you arrive at that estimation?*
Regardless of the method used to calculate the value of your business, you should ask what the estimation is based on. Business brokers should support estimated figures with evidence of recent sales of similar businesses within a comparable area.

15. *Do you assist with arranging financing?*
It is becoming more and more difficult to borrow money from banks, unless the seller has perfect books and records, and the buyer has near perfect credit, with 25–30 percent deposit, collateral to secure the loan, and industry experience. Therefore, you need to hire a business broker that understands this and has experience in arranging financing. Otherwise, your business is not going to sell.

16. *What marketing material will you provide to prospective buyers on my business?*

It is imperative to utilize a business broker that will write a complete information memorandum on your business, not just a listing on the Internet or a one-page business listing information.

17. *How and to whom will you market my business? (Will they just put ads up on the Internet?)*

You need to make sure you choose a business broker that puts together a creative marketing plan. Choose one that has a buyer database and does strategic marketing, not just Internet marketing.

Ask potential business brokers how they are going to advertise and get the word out about your business for sale. Make sure they allocate an adequate budget for advertising and marketing to sell your business.

18. *Who determines when and if you will spend money on marketing my business?*

Agents have no voice in how the owner of the business brokerage firm spends his or her money. Agents do not spend any advertising money on their listings; it is solely up to the firm's owners to determine which listings they spend money on. If you are dealing with the agent and not the owner, then get clarification on how much marketing and what type of marketing they are going to do on your business.

19. *How do you qualify buyers?*

Brokers need to qualify buyers, particularly before your business financials are given to them. It is a good idea that all buyers fill out a buyer package, which includes a financial statement. If the buyer is not willing to provide his or her financials, then the business broker should not provide the buyer with any information whatsoever on your business.

20. *Do you have relationships with lawyers, tax specialist accountants, and lenders?*

One of the main reasons that deals fall apart is because of loss of control over other professionals that are involved in the deal or the buyer's/seller's problems are not being solved in order to finalize the sale. The more relationships that the broker has with other key specialists, the fewer problems he or she will have in that particular deal.

COLLABORATION IS KEY

While it's true you can't make everyone work together, when you're working on your exit plan, it's ideal to have all your professionals work collaboratively. This might look like:

- *Show the exit plan.* To help create context for the professionals in your exit plan, it can help to show them the plan you have created. While they may not have an active role in all the parts, they should at least understand how their part fits into everything else. Plus, when everyone knows your goals and your direction, they can effectively support you in moving ahead.
- *Share information.* Again, it might not be possible to have everyone share information, but you should at least give permission (when possible and needed) to share relevant information with one another. This will build more teamwork and provide information in a way that keeps you from having to do all the work.

- *Meet together.* Whenever it's possible and necessary, try to get your exit-planning team together to talk about what's happening, what's going to happen next, etc. This doesn't have to be an in-person meet, but it should be something where you can talk to and hear the thoughts of one another in real time (conference call, Skype, etc.).
- *Provide regular updates.* The more updates you can provide to everyone on the team, the more the team might be encouraged to provide updates to one another. The more everyone knows, the more effective they can be in their tasks and ongoing activities.
- *Encourage contact between professionals.* While you can't make anyone do anything, you can encourage contact among the team members. Give the contact information to the professionals and encourage them to speak when they need certain pieces of information.
- *Get multiple opinions.* Be clear that you will be getting opinions from everyone on the team. Often, when people realize this is happening, they are more likely to offer their own opinion and insight to one another.

Since you need to have as many professionals on your side as possible, collaboration will ensure they are working together and not suggesting things that don't complement other activities. Know too that collaborating is a key role your exit planner will play in their relationship with you.

RESOURCES

Below is a checklist of the questions to help with selecting your team:

EXIT PLANNER

Have you asked these questions of your exit planner, and how did he or she respond?	1 = Not Good 5 = Good
1. What are your qualifications?	
2. What kind of clients do you see, and what services do you provide? Do you have any specialties?	
3. What do you mean by "exit planning"?	
4. What do you do when you create an exit plan? Where do you start?	
5. What do you include in your exit plans? Can you show me an example of a plan you have created?	
6. Are you able to assist in finding out what my business is worth?	
7. Assuming that my business is not worth enough today to support the lifestyle I want when I exit, what will you do for me?	
8. Who will be involved in this plan?	
9. Who will look after my business most of the time? Who will be doing the work?	
10. How do you work alongside my other business advisers?	
11. Once you create my plan, what will we do if circumstances change?	
12. If I decide to transfer my company to my key employees (or child), and I know they don't have any money, what ideas do you have to handle that?	
13. I want to sell to a third party. What do buyers look for? Can you help me improve my business to make it attractive to owners?	
14. What happens to my company and family if I don't live to see my exit date?	

Have you asked these questions of your exit planner, and how did he or she respond?	1 = Not Good 5 = Good
15. How do you invoice for your services? Is it done monthly, biannually?	
16. What sort of access will I be given to the data you hold about my business?	
17. Can you provide business advice and assist in the financial management of my business?	
18. Are you available year-round?	
19. How much contact do you have with your clients?	
20. Do you have testimonials?	
21. Did he or she ask me questions and seem to be interested in me?	

FINANCIAL PLANNER

Have you asked these questions of your financial planner, and how did he or she respond?	1 = Not Good 5 = Good
1. What licenses, credentials, or other certifications do you have?	
2. What services do you/does your firm provide?	
3. How do you charge for your services, and how much?	
4. What types of clients do you specialize in?	
5. Could I see a sample financial plan?	
6. What is your investment approach?	
7. How much contact do you have with your clients?	
8. Will I be working only with you or with a team?	
9. What makes your client experience unique?	
10. Did he or she ask me questions and seem to be interested in me?	

LAWYER

Have you asked these questions of your lawyer, and how did he or she respond?	1 = Not Good 5 = Good
1. What are your qualifications, and how much experience do you have with my industry?	
2. What is your approach to conflict resolution?	
3. Who will look after my business most of the time? How many partners are there? Will there be anyone else handling my work?	
4. What kind of clients do you see most often?	
5. Do you have any clients who could create conflicts?	
6. What is your communication style? How long do you typically take to get back to people?	
7. How do you invoice for your services?	
8. Are there ways to reduce the cost of your services?	
9. Do you belong to any specialized bar associations?	
10. Do you make referrals to other lawyers?	

TAX PROFESSIONAL

Have you asked these questions of your tax professional, and how did he or she respond?	1 = Not Good 5 = Good
1. What are your qualifications? Do you have experience with taxes?	
2. How long has the practice been operating, and how long have you been with the practice?	
3. What kind of clients do you see, and what services do you provide?	
4. What other services do you provide? Do you have expertise in areas relevant to me?	
5. Will you represent me if I am audited?	

Have you asked these questions of your tax professional, and how did he or she respond?	1 = Not Good 5 = Good
6. How do you keep track of changes in a client's circumstances?	
7. Who will look after my business most of the time? Who will be doing the work? What is the size of the practice?	
8. Are you a conservative or more aggressive tax professional?	
9. How do you handle working with multiple entities?	
10. How will your practice help me develop my business?	
11. What sort of access will I be given to the data you hold about my business?	
12. Can you provide business advice and assist in the financial management of my business?	
13. Will you return my calls within a reasonable time? How long will you take to complete your work?	
14. Are you available year-round?	
15. Are you familiar with the accounting/ software package I use in my business? What technology do you use?	
16. How will you communicate with me? How will I be informed, particularly of any changes to legislation?	

Have you asked these questions of your tax professional, and how did he or she respond?	1 = Not Good 5 = Good
17. How do you bill for your services, and what will I get for my money? • What does the project or subscription include? • Do they price each job before they start, so you can both agree to the scope and terms? • Do they allow you to pay by the month to spread the burden on cash flow? • Do they charge for each phone call or e-mail, or are these questions included? • Do they charge by the hour (and are therefore rewarded for being inefficient), or do they charge for the value that they provide?	
18. What can you do to keep the fees down?	
19. Will you review my past tax returns at no charge?	
20. Do I need a tax lawyer?	

BUSINESS BROKER

Have you asked these questions of your business broker, and how did he or she respond?	1 = Not Good 5 = Good
1. How many years have you been selling businesses?	
2. How many brokerage offices do you have or are you affiliated with? Do you cobroker?	
3. How many businesses have you sold in your career in relation to the number of years you have been working as a broker?	
4. How many businesses do you sell a year?	
5. How long does an average sale take?	
6. What industries have you sold businesses in?	
7. How many listings do you have?	

Have you asked these questions of your business broker, and how did he or she respond?	1 = Not Good 5 = Good
8. Do you have a database of buyers? If so, how many?	
9. Do you have testimonials?	
10. What can I expect in regards to the level of communication from you?	
11. What does the listing agreement/contract include? What is your service charge? Is it negotiable?	
12. What is your success rate (closing ratio) in the last twelve months?	
13. How do you evaluate what my business is worth? What resources will you utilize to evaluate my business?	
14. What is your estimation of selling price? How did you arrive at that estimation?	
15. Do you assist with arranging financing?	
16. What marketing material will you provide to prospective buyers on my business?	
17. How and to whom will you market my business? (Will they just put ads up on the Internet?)	
18. Who determines when and if you will spend money on marketing my business?	
19. How do you qualify buyers?	
20. Do you have relationships with lawyers, tax specialist accountants, and lenders?	

VALUING YOUR BUSINESS

Price is what you pay. Value is what you get.

—Warren Buffett

When it comes to valuing your business, you might have a little bit of emotional attachment in the process. Your business is something you have worked hard to build, and you may truly believe the business is worth more than the market says it is. Most entrepreneurs are very much like homeowners. Entrepreneurs and homeowners almost always think the property is worth more than it really is. That's human nature. However, all emotion must be put aside before you can successfully value a business.

When you're looking at selling your company, you need to take the emotional blinkers off and begin to see what your company actually offers the market in terms of value. Even if you find out that the value of your company is less than you think it is, know there are ways to help increase its overall value and its overall price when it's sold.

Even though it might seem like value is a number you can clearly define, this is far from the case. Remember that value is precisely what a person is willing to spend to buy something. After all, if someone wants to spend one million dollars on buying your company, that's its value—even if it's worth only one hundred thousand.

Value can be a bit subjective in that way, but that's a good thing. If you're able to show that your company is worth more than what it appears, then you can get more during a sale to an investor or organization.

But you have to start the conversation about value somewhere, and that means you need to do some math to figure out what your company's price might be right now.

KNOW YOUR WORTH

The first question to consider is: what is the value of your business?

SETTING THE VALUE

It is important to understand how the value of your business can be set and the details you should consider. With all the different approaches to assessing the value of a business, the more you understand about the different methodologies, the more you will be able to understand your company's role in the process.

For those who are new to the process of selling a company, it may not be necessary to be an expert in the methodologies, but it will be necessary to have some understanding of how others are looking at your company.

Although there are a number of different valuation methods you can use, there is no exact answer on the best method to use.

It is important to do your own research and get advice from your exit planner and business broker. The five most commonly used valuation methods are:

- discounted cash flow
- capitalized future earnings
- earnings multiple
- asset valuation
- comparable sale

Discounted Cash Flow and Capitalized Future Earnings

These two methods are the most common methods used to value small businesses. They are often used because they can be applied to businesses in a number of industries. When you sell your business, you are selling its assets and the right to all future profits or cash flow. Both methods consider the rate of return the investor can expect to get from the business.

Capitalized Future Earnings:

$$\text{Value} = \frac{\text{Average net profit over the past three years adjusted for one-off expenses or other irregular items in each year}}{\text{Expected rate of return}}$$

There are no fixed rules on the rate of return that is used. The rate will be driven by the expected risk in your business and comparable other investments.

Discounted Cash Flow:

Future free cash flow projections are discounted using the weighted average cost of capital to arrive at a present value. The formula to calculate the discounted cash flow is:

$$\text{Discounted Cash Flow} = \frac{\text{CF Year 1}}{(1 + DR)} + \frac{\text{CF Year 2}}{(1 + DR)^2} + \frac{\left[\dfrac{\text{CF Year 3}}{(DR - G)} \right]}{(1 + DR)^2}$$

CF = Cash Flow forecast
DR = Discount Rate based on weighted average cost of capital
G = Expected Growth rate in perpetuity

Discounted cash flow models are powerful and can be complex.

Earnings Multiple

The value is calculated by multiplying the earnings before interest and tax (EBIT) by a multiplier. The multiplier depends on the industry your business is in, the growth potential of your business, and other risk factors the investor considers relevant.

The ten value factors discussed in the next section explain the factors investors take into account when setting the multiplier. These factors also impact on the expected rate of return and discount rate used in the two valuation methods discussed above.

An established business with sustainable profits might sell for as much as six times the earnings, while a service-based business might be valued for as little as one times the earnings.

Asset Valuation

Another way to determine the value of your company is to calculate its net assets.

This method determines what your business would be worth if it were closed today and the assets were sold, by adding the fair value of the assets less the liabilities. Assets might include everything from real estate you own to the inventory you have, etc. These are all the items your company has in its possession (i.e., things that could be sold for money).

It doesn't take into account the liability of the assets to generate future profits and consequently doesn't take any goodwill into account. The asset valuation could undervalue your business.

This approach is often used for businesses that use a lot of assets to generate income (e.g., plant hire companies).

Goodwill can be described as the difference between the true value of your business and the value of its net assets.

If you have a service-based or retail business where there are not a lot of assets, it can be crucial to the value of your business to have goodwill included. For example, if you have a restaurant where service, reputation, and location are key factors, the value of any goodwill should be added to the net assets to get a valuation of your business.

If your business performance has been poor and has no goodwill, then using next asset valuation could be an accurate way to value your business.

Comparable Sales

Irrespective of the method you use, you should also look at prices from recent sales of similar businesses. Your business broker can assist you with providing insight into the market, as he or she will know what similar businesses are selling for and how the market is currently valuing businesses.

You can also check business-for-sale listings in industry magazines, newspapers, and websites.

In the end, the market determines the value of your company, but you can also tell the market what you are worth by proving your potential. When you can prove to outside investors and market professionals that your business is worth more than the numbers might indicate, you may be able to get the price you want.

You can begin to show others you are worth more than the market tells you by showing potential investors:

- *What similar companies have sold for.* Again, showing investors what other buyers have paid for similar companies will help you leverage your company's sale. At the same time, this may not always work in your favor, as some of these sales may not have resulted in profits. Choose your comparable wisely. Your business broker can be of great assistance in preparing the comparatives for you. You should keep in mind that prospective buyers will do their own investigations into what other companies have sold for, so be prepared to be challenged on the comparatives you provide.
- *What your financial forecast looks like.* If you can take the numbers from the entire history of your company and show that you have made more money each year, an investor will be able to see the potential of your company and its future.

Though this, again, does not guarantee anything, the data will help to prove the trends in your company, and it will help to add perceived value to your company.

Of course, you will need to be a company that actually makes money and has a history of making money. You will want to have an established pattern of success, or else it will not be clear what your value is in the market and what your value in the market could be.

But what does this mean? For many smaller businesses, the average range of a business sale might be one to two times the adjusted earnings, or it might be much higher if it is possible the company could have larger profits and growth in the future.

It is a slippery process to be sure, and the valuation of your company might just be a matter of timing on your part. If the market at a certain point thinks your company is worth a lot, then you might be able to sell at a better price than if the market simply isn't focused on buying companies.

Even with all the information you might have and all the information you might see in the market, you may still need to hope for the best when it comes to your company's sale.

Setting the value of your company can be complex, and your advisers should assist you in the process. Using your advisers will also ensure an objective value is set, and getting that independence is strongly recommended.

GETTING THE NUMBERS

To compile the numbers you need for a valuation, it is helpful to think about what your business plan included. When you can show these types of details to potential investors, they will be able to see where you are headed—and where the company is likely to go.

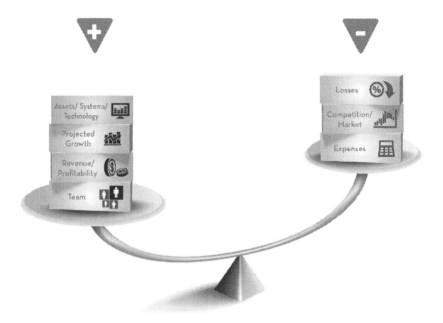

- *Assets*. In this section of your report on your value, you will want to list all the things you have in your company that are owned by you or that are a part of your company's production activities. This might include: computers, equipment, vehicles, real estate, work sites, etc. All the things that you own as a company should be a part of this list.

- *Expenses*. Since expenses can vary depending on what you are doing and what you plan to do next, it's a good idea to list the expected expenses, based on the last few years of growth. Make a detailed list of what you spend your money on in the company and be clear about how this helps your company in its growth.

- *Team*. While it might not seem like your team adds to your value, the more expertise you have at your company, the more you will add to the effectiveness of your company's activities. You can list out the management structure, as well as your team's skill sets, to showcase the value of your team.

- *Revenue.* You will want to have the revenue reports from the entire history of your company, including what you made each year, each month, and even in smaller segments if necessary. This will help to show that you have a positive cash flow, assuming you do!

- *Losses.* In addition, you will need to state your losses, as every company will have these. The more honest you are in your reporting, the more you will instill trust, and the more you will show the investors that you understand how to manage the ups and downs of business ownership.

- *Projected growth.* Projecting the growth of your company will help to increase the value of your company. If you can show that your company is trending upward, then you can project the same type of growth in the next five to ten years. While the impressiveness of the growth is dependent on what has already happened, growth of any kind will help to increase the interest of investors.

- *Competition/market.* By detailing the competition and what their revenue/profitability patterns have been, you can show how you rate and how you relate to the rest of the market. It might be that you are similar to other businesses, but you have shown steadier growth, which is far more appealing to intelligent investors.

The more you can show about your value, both inferred and factual, the more you will assign a value to your company. Note that if you're not profitable yet, it is very difficult to show an investor that you have the potential to be profitable, except if you have a new product or patent that will be a hit in the market.

If you're still in the growing stages, wait a little bit longer to start citing a value for your company.

WHY VALUE MATTERS

Value matters in every arena of business, as you've no doubt suspected and learned. When your company has a higher value, or even a perceived higher value, you will be able to:

- *Receive greater interest in your company.* It makes sense that the more value your company has (or is perceived to have), the more others will be interested in your company. This interest extends beyond potential buyers and investors to customers. The more your company is seen as being a leader, the more others will want to be a part of your company's success.
- *Sell it for a higher price.* Of course, the more value your company is perceived to have, the more you will be able to get for it when you decide to sell it to someone else.
- *Encourage bidding wars.* In an ideal world, the improved value would also increase the interest of other companies, helping to encourage bidding wars, which will increase the sales price by a larger percentage.
- *Improve your company's image.* The more your company is seen as having value, the more your company will be seen as valuable in the market. In terms of helping to guarantee the long-term success of your company, perceived value can do a lot for even the smallest company.
- *Preserve your company's long-term value.* While you may not be a part of the company for much longer, you do want the company to be successful for the rest of the team. With a higher value number, the company will be seen as being continued competition.

Though none of this information is surprising to most business owners, it makes sense to remember that value does add up to more than just money. Value helps to equate the business with success, which can add up to increased revenue in the future, less competition, etc.

The more you can build the value of your company, the more all stakeholders will be able to reap in the process.

FROM THE INVESTOR POINT OF VIEW

You may have keen business sense and an ability to understand what your market needs, but that doesn't always make you the best person to understand what an investor wants. This is why you might call in a business broker and an exit planner to help you with this part of your exit plan.

At the same time, the more you can get into the mind of the investor, the more you can do right now to help improve the value of your company, the more you can do to entice the investor to make an offer for your business, and the more you can encourage higher offers.

WHAT THEY WANT TO KNOW

When your company is being pursued in a sale, you might notice you are nervous around investors. They seem as though they are looking at everything, and you are concerned they will find the smallest reason to not purchase your company.

It is all true.

But when you can think about what they want to know, you can begin to understand why they scrutinize everything in your business.

- *They prefer to make money.* Think about it. If you were going to spend a few million dollars on a company, you want to make sure you're getting something in return.
- *They don't want to lose money.* At the very least, you would hope that you wouldn't lose money in a million-dollar purchase.

- *They may be representing someone else, and they need to please their interests and concerns.* Some investors have to please someone else, so they're not necessarily looking for something wrong in your company. They are, however, making sure they have seen everything so they can make a complete report back to the person or organization that hired them.
- *They many have had bad experiences in the past with buying companies.* When an investor has not had a good track record of success in the past, he or she might be a bit pickier during the evaluation of a company.
- *They want to make sure they're getting the best price.* Yes, this needs to be repeated. Investors need to know they're getting the best price. They don't want to spend a cent more than they have to spend, even if it's a highly valuable company.

Investors just want to know they are going to make money from the deal. While they might also care about helping another company out, or helping you out in particular, if they're not getting a good deal, they're not going to be interested in what your company has to offer.

WHAT THEY NEED TO KNOW

Investors need to know a few things when they're looking to buy companies. While numbers are going to help support this information, there are some things that can't be quantified as easily. These are some of the things investors need to know:

- *The company will succeed.* Though nothing is ever 100 percent certain, investors want to be pretty certain that the company will succeed. After all, if they spend a lot of money on something that isn't going to give them any return, what is the point of that investment?
- *The company has succeeded.* A track record of success is often what an investor will use to measure the anticipated success

for the company. An upward trend in sales that is better than industry or market trends will indicate future upward trends or at least the propensity for increased revenue. An upward trend in sales in isolation is by itself not a good indicator of performance and should always be compared against how the market or industry sectors are performing. Likewise, outside forces could cause a flat or even a slight dip in the market, and having some growth in these circumstances is a good indication of potential future success.

- *The company is set up for success.* Investors will also look at the structure of the company and analyze it carefully. In doing so, they will be able to see if there are areas in which the company still needs to improve, or if there are areas in which things are working well. The more the company is already set up for success, the less the investor will need to do at the start to keep the company profitable.

- *The company is in a market that needs them.* While markets are always changing, and it's hard to know what the market might want next, the company needs to at least be in a market that has potential for growth and sustainable revenue generation. If the market seems to be moving in a new direction, but the company is not, then the investor may not be as interested in making that purchase.

- *Customers are interested and loyal.* The customer base can often predict the value of a company far more than numbers can. When the customers are devoted to a company, they will come back again and again. They will spend their money and be willing to continue to buy new products because they trust the company. This adds to the value of the company, and it increases the overall viability of the investment.

Investors who are representing companies may also want to know more about the existing technology, the systems, etc., that are in place, depending on the needs of the company and of the organization.

- *What technology is being used.* When a company doesn't have the latest technology available, the investor will have to update that technology, often at a great cost. If your business is lagging behind on technology, the question should be asked as to whether replacing the technology would have a greater increase in the selling price than the cost of the replacement. If the cost to replace the technology is more than the perceived value, it is recommended to minimize the investment. However, from an investor's perspective, it might be less risky to find a company that already has everything in place and already has the things necessary for success. Technology projects have a reputation of being over budget and over time, and the investor might not have the appetite to take on this risk. Knowing the competition in the market when you are looking to sell will provide insight into whether or not to make the investment.
- *What systems are in place.* Since having good systems increases productivity and efficiency, investors may look at the systems the company already uses. While they might compare them to the systems they already know, the more the company can prove their systems are effective, the more value the company will have. There will be fewer things to change and to adjust.
- *Who the team is.* The investor may buy a company and keep all the existing team members. When this is the case, the investor will need to know who the team members are, what they have to offer, and how they are better than other workers that could be brought in as replacements.

Investors are looking at everything, kicking every tire in the company to ensure they are getting their money's worth (while not spending a cent more than they have to).

By thinking like an investor, you may already be able to see where your company needs to make some changes in order to be more attractive to the prospective buyer.

THE TEN VALUE FACTORS

There are ten factors that will make your company more attractive and increase the sale price through the multiple or discount rate the buyer would be willing to offer, aside from financial performance. These ten factors all focus on reducing the business risk for the buyer:

1. *Growth potential.* If a company has the ability and the market in which to become larger than it is right now, it will affect the value. After all, a company that is destined to make more money in the future is more appealing.
2. *Number of customers/clients.* If a company is reliant on one customer or primarily one customer, this can negatively impact the value and salability. Should the customer decide to leave in the future, it would cause the company significant revenue loss.
3. *Cash flow/profitability.* It matters how the cash flow and the profitability figures move in relation to each other. The goal should be to have a company that continues to create a positive cash flow rather than one that continues to move up and down.
4. *Recurring revenue.* In this arena, companies that can clearly show how they will continue to have a source of revenue are going to be more attractive and have a higher value.
5. *Product monopoly.* This means your company is one that sells or offers something that few other companies do. In this situation, your company's protective "moat" will not be easily breached by the competition.

6. *Customer satisfaction.* Of course, the happier your customers are, the more value your company will have to a buyer.

7. *Owner dependence.* A company that can thrive without its owner is one that is more valuable to a buyer. You need to be a part of the company's growth but also a part of ensuring it will grow without you on the team.

8. *Management team.* A company that has a management team that can share the load of responsibility is often seen as more valuable to a prospective buyer.

9. *Age of company.* Though the time a company is open doesn't always measure its chance for success, it does mean that it has a more solid foundation than a company that has just begun.

10. *Long-term plans.* When a company, for example, has spent a lot of time and money on research, it might be setting itself up for long-term growth, which will be more attractive to an investor than a company that has not considered what might happen next.

As you can see, there are a number of other potential factors to consider in the valuation of your company—and factors an investor will consider. The more you can focus on improving these ten factors, the higher the value you will receive.

The more you can identify what might be important to a specific investor, the more you can offer proof to show the value of your company.

BUILDING VALUE

Like anything you own, there are ways you can increase the value of your business in order to make it more attractive to investors and to encourage a higher price in the market.

During your exit planning, it's best to start thinking about these value-building strategies as soon as possible so they have time to do what they are meant to do, and so that you can increase the value as much as possible before you make the eventual sale to the investor. Chapter 4 discusses in detail the fourteen value enhancement strategies to consider.

Value is certainly dependent on the market and on factors you can't control, but there are proven ways to increase your company's value and increase the profit you would make from its sale before you leave and move into retirement.

WHAT YOU CAN DO NOW

The biggest question on your mind right now is probably, what can I do now? It is a question that you will want to address with the help and support of a professional. You need to start finding the answers.

Right now, your goals need to include the following steps:

- *Find out what you have.* Determine what you already have in place that will support you in reaching your exit-planning goals.
- *Find out what you need to have in place.* Identify the gaps in your plan and what you need to put into place in order to reach your long-term and short-term goals.
- *Choose the best professionals to help you in your journey.* Look at the options you have for professional help and start considering what they have to offer you and your strategy.
- *Identify how you will transition from your position at your company.* Decide whether you will simply leave the company on a certain date, if you will take on another role, or if you will have a more gradual transition to retirement.
- *Seek out the best buyer for your business.* Start looking at people who might be interested in buying your company and start marketing your company to them.
- *Increase the value of your business by identifying the key business drivers.* To enhance the appeal of your business, identify and celebrate the key business drivers in your company. Key business drivers are discussed below.
- *Improve your overall systems and documentation.* While you are in the process of selling your company and/or transferring ownership, find ways to improve the systems you already have in place. You want to make things stronger for the next person who will be at the helm of your company.
- *Sell your business.* Once you find the right buyer and the right price, you will move through the process of selling your company, with the help of a lawyer, business broker, and exit planner.
- *Enjoy your life, however that looks.*

KEY BUSINESS DRIVERS

Key business drivers are items that can increase the value of a product or service by improving the perception of the item and essentially providing a competitive advantage. Drivers can come in many forms, such as cutting-edge technology, brand recognition, or satisfied customers.

The ten value factors described above are what can make your company more attractive in terms of its value and its price in the eyes of a prospective buyer. You also want to know what can drive this value.

The more you know, the more you can do, after all.

What are business-value drivers?
Some examples of business drivers include:

- competition
- customer diversity
- customer satisfaction
- financial history
- financial strength
- loyal employees
- management depth
- owner involvement
- proprietary technology
- proprietary processes
- patents and trademarks

Keep in mind that the business drivers might be different, depending on the industry. For example, if you're in retail, you might look at your inventory management and your sales team, but when you're in another industry, you will only need to look at how you manage relationships or how you offer customer service to your audience.

The business driver is the thing or many things that set your business apart. What you may not have realized is that your business plan already began to identify a process you can use to find the unique drivers for your business: the SWOT analysis—a list of strengths, weaknesses, opportunities, and threats, which can help in the analysis of a business during planning or exit planning. All business owners should complete the various aspects of the SWOT analysis.

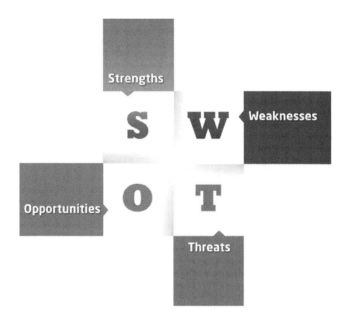

Let's break this down right now so you can get a better sense of how to use this tool in order to find the business-value drivers that will set you apart from others.

Strengths
- What does your company do well?
- How does your company serve its customers effectively?
- What systems have improved efficiency?
- What products are getting a lot of attention?
- What successes has your company already seen in its time being open?

- What does your talent bring to the table?
- What makes you better than everyone else?
- What does your revenue look like?

Weaknesses

- What does your company not do well right now?
- How does your company not serve its customers effectively?
- What systems have reduced efficiency?
- What products aren't getting a lot of attention?
- What products or services have failed?
- What weaknesses has your company already seen in its time being open?
- What is missing in your staff and management team?
- What makes you less competitive?
- What do your losses or debts look like?

Opportunities

- What can your company add to its products and/or services?
- What audience has your company not looked into yet?
- What marketing tools have you explored?
- What are some suggestions you have received from your audience?
- What do you feel you can do that your competition can't or has not done?
- What are some ways you can grow?

Threats

- What products or services aren't serving your financial health?
- What audiences have not responded or have turned away?
- What marketing tools are you not using?
- What is your competition doing that you can't do?
- Is your market oversaturated? Does it have the possibility to become oversaturated in the future?

- What are some ways you can't get any bigger?
- What impact will new technology have on your industry?

The more you can look at the way your company works and doesn't work, the more you can identify what you do well.

WHO CAN HELP

When it comes to valuing your company, the best person to ask might be someone who doesn't already know what your company does, but they know how to assess what your company has done. This might include a legal professional, a business broker, an exit planner, etc.

You want to reach out to people who provide valuations for companies and see if they can perform an audit to see what your company has to offer. Though it's true you might get different answers, depending on who you ask to look at the value of your company, the more information you have, the more you will know.

Let's look at the main items an outside professional should consider in a valuation of your company:

- true profit
- net tangible assets
- future sustainable profits
- future cash flow
- business risk

If you look at this information, you can see how a financial professional (i.e., an accountant) might be the best person for the job. They can take the numbers you have provided about your business and begin to speculate about what your future might look like in the company.

From there, they can extrapolate your company's value to someone who is making the purchase.

RESOURCES

The following checklists will help you prepare for the sale of your business.

ANSWERING INVESTOR QUESTIONS

Are you comfortable that you can confidently answer the following questions investors will want answers to?	1 = Not Good 5 = Good
How likely is the company to succeed?	
How is the company set up to ensure success in the future?	
How is the company positioned in the market?	
Is customer satisfaction and loyalty evident?	
What technology is in place?	
What systems are in place?	
What team is in place?	

TEN VALUE FACTORS THAT WILL IMPACT THE PRICE

Have you addressed the following ten factors in your business?	1 = Not Good 5 = Good
1. Growth potential	
2. Number of customers/clients	
3. Cash flow/profitability	
4. Recurring revenue	
5. Product monopoly	
6. Customer satisfaction	
7. Owner dependence	
8. Management team	
9. Age of company	
10. Long-term plans	

4

HOW TO INCREASE YOUR BUSINESS VALUE—THE FOURTEEN VALUE ENHANCERS

Business is a game, played for fantastic stakes, and you're in competition with experts. If you want to win, you have to learn to be a master of the game.

— Sydney Sheldon, *Master of the Game*

In this chapter, you will learn how you can increase the value of your company using a simple fourteen-step process so you can earn more from the sale and set the company up for long-term success. Finally, by creating a business plan, investors can easily see what your company has to offer and whether it is something that will enhance their goals or if they need to look elsewhere for a company that is more in line with their long-term strategy.

When you want to make more money on the sale of your business, you need to be ready and willing to take steps to increase its value. While these steps might seem extensive and even more time-consuming than running your business, they are also setting your company up for long-term success.

And that equals value to a prospective buyer.

The fourteen steps are:

> *Step 1: Make your business attractive.* Create street appeal for your business, making potential investors more interested to look at the business.

Step 2: Increase your profits. Profit is one of the key drivers in valuing a business and the key to having a positive cash flow.

Step 3: Document the things people can't see. Investors will only pay for what they can see.

Step 4: Clear your debts. Investors normally are not interested in taking on the debt of the previous owners.

Step 5: Promote your positive cash flow. Cash is king, and a positive cash flow will always attract a premium from investors.

Step 6: *Organize your books.* During the due diligence process, your books will be looked at with a fine-tooth comb, and if there are any discrepancies, it will impact negatively on all the other information provided to the buyer.

Step 7: Create systems. Well-defined and documented systems assure investors that they will be able to walk in and run the operations of the business.

Step 8: Get yourself out of the way. A business that is heavily reliant on the owner to operate is a risk to any buyer, as the owner is not going to be there after the sale.

Step 9: Continue to work. As an owner, you need to make the business less dependent on you while at the same time driving the changes that are needed in the business to increase the value.

Step 10: Get your affairs settled. A clean business with no hanging issues (e.g., legal cases) assures the buyer that he or she can focus on the future rather than having to deal with issues from the past.

Step 11: Update your business. A business that appears to be modern and that has kept up with the times means the buyer does not have to invest effort to modernize the business.

Step 12: Improve your talent. A talented and stable team is difficult to build.

Step 13: Set up a business plan. Business plans provide a clear summary to the investor of where the value is in the business.

Step 14: Qualify prospective buyers. Approaching buyers that will derive more benefit from your business (e.g., increase their market share and therefore reduce competition) will always be willing to pay more than an investor who is only looking to make a return on an investment.

STEP 1: MAKE YOUR BUSINESS ATTRACTIVE

If you're looking at a new house, what's the first thing you see when you walk up to the door? You see everything that's happening on the outside of the house. An unkempt lawn can make it seem as though the owner doesn't care about the property, and many prospective buyers won't even look at the inside of the house.

Your business is much the same way. When prospective buyers are looking at your business, they want to see how it appeals from the outside as much as it does from the inside.

You can increase your company's curb appeal by doing the following:

- *Find out what your company looks like in the market.* If you don't already know what your company looks like in your local market, you need to find out—and quickly. Take surveys of your customers to see what they think, what they like, what they don't like, etc. Look at your website from an outsider's perspective; see what works and what doesn't. Look very carefully at your company, as though you were trying to buy it. Would you be interested in it or would you feel it wasn't a good investment?

- *Seek out criticism.* While it might not be the most exciting part of this process, you should try to find people and customers who were not happy with their experiences. The more you can learn about the negative things in your company, the more you can make sure you're making changes that have an impact on the people who give you money for your products and services.

- *Increase brand positioning.* If your overall brand isn't getting the attention it deserves, or your brand strategy was working for a while, but now it's not, it's time to rethink your brand. Find out where you are positioned in the market and how you might be better placed. Maybe the way your company looked in the past was effective, but now your company needs freshening up to keep up with the competition. In advertising, you tweak a brand to freshen it and then carry the tweak forward into the ad campaign. The home page of a website needs to change often to maintain its "freshness." Look at the competition to see how you can set yourself apart. After all, if you seem like everyone else, what's there to make you seem special and worth the investment?

- *Start community outreach.* While you might not be a local company, the more you can do for your local community, through your company, the more credibility you will have in the market. Since many companies have focused only on what they have sold and not on how they are seen, you can give yourself an advantage. Differentiating yourself as a good corporate citizen provides an inherent value to the business. Creating an image as a good corporate citizen is a long-term effort. It can't be done overnight.

- *Share your company's successes.* Sometimes it's hard to see what the value of a company is, especially when the company doesn't talk about the things it's done. While you don't need to boast about everything, you do want to make sure the good things you have done are being seen. This might include testimonials from clients, success stories, research, etc. The more you can show that your company is doing good things, the more investors will want to be a part of your success.

Think about what your company looks like to the people who don't know anything about it and who don't go any deeper than what they see at first glance. This will help you to better understand what investors actually see and why they might not be coming in the proverbial door to learn more.

STEP 2: INCREASE YOUR PROFITS

It's not surprising that increasing your profits will help you increase your overall value. No matter what size business you are, you need to find ways to improve your revenue. True, this makes good business sense, no matter what stage of ownership you are in, but it's even more important when you want to get an investor interested in what you have to say.

To increase your profits, you need to find ways to bring customers in the door and to have them return more often than they might have in the past. You can accomplish this by doing the following:

- *Find out what your customers want.* Though you may already have a successful company and business, you have to keep asking your customers what they want so you are certain you are delivering. People's needs change, and they will go elsewhere if you can't meet their needs. Having regular surveys can help you spot new trends and possible ways to grow your company's profits. (Just make sure there's a benefit to filling out the survey so you get more results—for example, a discount on a future purchase.)

- *Meet the needs of loyal customers.* It's said that it is most expensive and more difficult to find new customers than it is to please and retain loyal customers. Reach out to your long-term customers to find out if they're happy and how you can help. Calling them personally is a great way to make an impression, for example. You want to show those who have been adding to your profitability that you are happy they are there.

- *Seek out new customers/identify new markets.* At the same time, you can't keep all your customers forever. You need to find customers to replace them and to add to your bottom line. Reach out into new markets to see who your new target customers are and start a marketing conversation with them. Find out if they're interested in what you have to say and sell, and find out how you can support them in new ways too.

- *Improve your marketing strategy.* It's clear from the invention of social media and online marketing how messages can be delivered instantly when they're delivered over the Internet. With this power, it's clear you can't simply settle on what's worked in the past. You need to do more, and you need to say more and say it in the right places. To do this, you need to look at where you are getting responses in your marketing strategy and where you might want to put your time, energy, and attention. For example, if you notice that your Google ads aren't getting a lot of response, but your Facebook ads are, then you should spend more money on where your return on investment (ROI) is the highest.

- *Add recurring items.* You may also want to look for products you can add to your business as ways to increase your profits. These might include consumables (e.g., printer sale and recurring toner sales), subscriptions, contracts, automatic renewals, niche items, etc.
- *Adopt the 3X financial model.* You can grow your profit by double digits simply by adopting the 3X financial improvement model. How does it work?
  - Improve sales by 3 percent
  - Improve cost of sales by 3 percent
  - Improve overheads by 3 percent

It is a simple 3 percent improvement across three financial areas. For example:

	Now		After 3X	
Sales	$2,000,000		$2,060,000	
Cost of Sales	$1,600,000	80%	$1,586,000	77%
Margin	$400,000		$473,800	
Overheads	$60,000	15%	$56,856	12%
Profit	$340,000	17%	$416,944	20%
Profit Growth			$76,944	22.6%

Asking anyone in your team to grow sales by 3 percent and reduce costs by 3 percent, and the answer would be, "We can achieve that." The impact, however, is significant.

While you should be interested in ways to increase your overall profits, it should be said that you should do this in a positive way. Some companies might say they aren't paying their leaders a salary, as that will make their profits appear larger than they are.

Or some companies might reduce the cost of making their products while reducing the quality, which might work in the short term but is not conducive to long-term growth.

You already know how to grow your company, but it's time to make things even more successful when you want to sell the company to someone else who also wants to succeed as much as you have.

STEP 3: DOCUMENT THE THINGS PEOPLE CAN'T SEE

Even though many people don't give themselves enough credit, business owners have many more things of value than their profit reports. As a business owner, you have intangible things that might help investors feel even better about their decision.

These might include things like:

- *Proprietary research and formulas.* You may very well have done research into certain areas, helping to fuel your success and drive your overall business strategy. While you might not share these things immediately with everyone who might be interested in buying your company, they are certainly things that can add value. You might offer them as vague ideas to an interested investor, with the idea he or she would get the full information upon purchase of the company.
- *How you acquire new customers.* Some companies simply get new customers easily; it almost seems effortless. But what many people don't realize is that this effortlessness comes from years of creating and testing out customer acquisition strategies. Your secret recipe for getting customers may be quite valuable to the investor, as he or she will simply use it and see the same results. The investor doesn't have to make

up anything new to generate what you have already been able to generate on your own.

- *How you evaluate locations.* If you're a company that has to evaluate real estate locations or other sites, you may have come up with a formula to do this effectively. When this is the case, the investor can gain access to how to follow your prescription for success. (Note too that this might apply to things like evaluating clients, accounts, etc.)
- *How you satisfy a customer.* When you have a cutting-edge way to deal with customers, someone who is not a part of the everyday process or who is on the outside might not easily see these activities taking place. But for many successful companies, the way they treat their customers is what makes them success and what drives their revenue. If you have these tactics, you can also share these with investors to help them better understand how they too can make customers return again and again.
- *How you approach product strategies.* The more you show that you have grown your business with additional items for customers to buy and to add to your revenue, the more value you can prove to a buyer.

Think hard about the things you do that you may not have written down or that you may not have as a standard policy in the employee handbook. What are the things that have led to your success—things that you have done or that your team has developed?

Those are all things that can increase the value of your company and that can lead to the eventual increased sale price.

STEP 4: CLEAR YOUR DEBTS

Getting rid of as much debt as possible is another way to increase the value of your company. Just as it's advised that you get rid of your personal debt, the more debt you can get rid of today, the more appealing you will be to an investor.

So many companies have debt piled up, and that's often why they want to have someone else take on the responsibility. But since you want to make money from your sale, and you don't just want to make enough money to clear your debts, you need to be smarter—and that means making some sacrifices.

- *Find out what your debts are.* If you're not sure what your debt situation is, it's time to get honest about these numbers and how much of your budget they encompass. Start writing down all the debts you still owe and think about the payments you make toward these debts each month (if you do!).
- *Talk with vendors.* When you owe money to your vendors, it's a good idea to talk with them to see if you can settle those debts for a smaller, lump sum payment. In some cases, this might work in the vendor's favor, so you may want to ask. This is not always a successful strategy, but it is one that has worked for others, and it doesn't hurt to find out if it's possible.
- *Create payment plans.* If you can't negotiate lower repayments, then think about a payment system or schedule. This includes a payment you decide to submit each and every month, while also including a target date for the entire sum to be repaid. This will help you stay on track, and it will ensure you are heading toward a debt-free company.
- *Reduce extras.* Just like in your everyday life, when you have too many debts, you will need to look at where you can cut back in your company. Find out where your extra money might be, and then direct those funds toward your debt payments.

You might need to scale back for a while, which will increase the rate at which you become debt free. (And you might find out you don't miss any of the things you cut out.)

- *Eliminate unnecessary staff.* While no one wants to cut out extra team members, it might be something you need to consider when you're trying to eliminate your debts. If there are positions you can cut or reduce, you will want to do so as soon as possible. These cuts may not be long term, but they can help you to improve your overall cash flow while also helping you to make more efficient systems that require fewer workers.
- *Focus on debt payments.* Though it might not seem like a lot of fun, it's a better idea to focus on debt payments before anything else in your company. Even if you need a new piece of technology, get rid of your debt before you take on any more. You need to be able to show investors how you are able to make the tough decisions for your company's health and success.

To be clear, you may not be able to get your company's debt to zero and keep it there forever. That may not be realistic. However, the more you can reduce the overall debt in your company, the more you will be able to show you are able to manage your company's finances.

Plus, no one wants to walk into a company and have to clear up someone else's debt.

Note: Paying off and/or paying down debt can be a long process, so the earlier you can start before your anticipated exit, the better. It will allow you to see more results and to show more progress.

It is important to understand the different types of debt when deciding which debt to pay off first. For example, a one-time loan for a long-term capital improvement might look better than debt incurred to preorder inventory. Low-interest mortgage debt over the land and buildings is always better than an overdraft at a high interest rate to fund the day-to-day operations of the business. Investors are most adverse to short-term debt that is used to fund the running of the business, as opposed to debt that funds capital purchases.

The earlier you start, the more momentum you can create for the next person in your shoes. He or she might just continue the debt payment plan you have developed.

STEP 5: PROMOTE YOUR POSITIVE CASH FLOW

Cash is king for any investor. In order to ensure your company shows it's moving positively toward revenue and profits, you need to show how you manage your cash flow.

- *Show the numbers.* To ensure buyers have all the information they need, you will want to show the cash flow of your company. This is the money in, the money out, and the difference between these two figures. If you are making money, the number will be positive, and if you are not making money, the number will be negative when you subtract the expenses/costs from your incoming monies. If the cash flow is negative, the exit plan should have clear strategies for how the cash flow will be turned around. It is not recommended to look at exiting the business while cash flow is negative, except if there is a clear plan showing how and when cash flow will be positive.
- *Reveal your strategy.* One way to help bring a positive spin on your cash flow is to talk about what you have done in order to maintain a positive cash flow. This will reveal the systems you have in place for maintaining a healthy company.
- *Explain times when things were not positive.* At the same time, if you don't have a consistently positive cash flow, then you

will need to talk about what you are doing to bring things back into balance. In addition, it's helpful to talk about when you believe the flow will be positive again.

Money does matter when it comes to the sale of your company. While it's true you don't have to be perfect, you do have to show you're striving for better.

STEP 6: ORGANIZE YOUR BOOKS

While many companies may think their books are in order, this is often not the case. Unless you've had your books managed by a professional accountant or bookkeeper, you will want to have someone else come in and help you out when you're preparing to sell your company.

- *Hire a professional.* No matter how good you've been with your books in the last few years, you may need to have a professional look at your numbers. They will know what to look for, and they're not going to be attached to the outcome, as you might be. Find professionals who have helped businesses similar to yours and who have cleaned up books for companies who are preparing to be sold.
- *Find your receipts.* To help your financial professional, start looking for all the receipts and financial paperwork you have for your company. Organize this as best you can, or at least be available to the bookkeeper or accountant on the day(s) he or she is setting up your new books. This will help you both understand what is there and what you might be missing.
- *Determine the best categories.* As you set up new systems, think about the best categories in which to file things. This will help you and the professional understand what is being listed and what it means at one glance. You want to make sure

you're keeping things as clear as possible when you are trying to entice the investor to your company.

- *Review the results*. Once you have all the financial facts ahead of you, start looking at the results to see what they say. Ask questions of your bookkeeper or accountant and make sure you understand every line of the report. If something doesn't look right, ask about it and ask how it might look to someone else. The more you look at your books in that way, the more you will be able to see what others are seeing.

- *Listen to recommendations*. If the bookkeeper or accountant has recommendations for you, take them into consideration. This is especially true when you haven't managed your books properly in a while. If the books need to be cleaned up, especially where "private" expenses are part of business expenses, it might take some time to correct this and show a track record of clean business accounts. This could delay any campaign for the sale of the business.

- *Get a second opinion*. Even after you've prepared and organized your books, it never hurts to have someone else look at them again to make sure everything is in order. Ideally, you will want to hire people who have no affiliation with your company. This way, you will be able to know their assessments and their figures are accurate.

- *Separate family and business expenses*. It's ideal that you separate your family expenses from the business expenses. In some small and family-run businesses, this can get a little confusing, and it can often showcase some less than admirable actions. For example, some business owners put family expenses through the business to save taxes, but this impacts the profit of the company, which will result in a lower price. When the owner leaves, the expenses will no longer be there, and the new owner will benefit from the cost saving.

The books you keep can show a company that is organized and prepared for success, or they can prove you haven't been tracking your finances. The more you can focus on creating order, the more order others will see in your company.

And a well-run company always keeps its books organized.

In addition, remember that the more organized you have things now, the easier it will be for a new investor to step into the organization. They don't want to have to clean anything up, and they don't want to have to manage any financial issues that arise unexpectedly.

STEP 7: CREATE SYSTEMS

When you're the person who's in charge of your company and what happens behind the scenes, you notice things that your customers may never see. This is mostly due to the fact that the processes you have put into place are processes that you created and designed.

But even with the best possible processes, there might be opportunities for improvement. When you can improve things, you have a greater opportunity for increased productivity, efficiency, and customer service.

To begin to identify areas of improvement:

- *List all your processes*. You can't see what you need to update until you start to list all the processes you have in place at your company. This can be overwhelming, so think about what happens when you arrive at your business, what you and your staff do all day, what you do when things go wrong, and what you do to close up. These are the processes. You might also have documentation processes, HR practices, etc., to include in this list.

- *Write out all the steps.* Once you have a (mostly) comprehensive list of what your activities look like, you can begin to list all the steps that are required to complete the activities. Write out these steps as though you are explaining them to someone who has no idea what they mean or what your company does. The more explicit and detailed you can be, the better. You want to identify every step and every possible step a staff member might take to complete this task.

- *Ask for staff feedback and adjustments.* After you have these documents in hand, send them to your staff, and especially to those who actually perform those tasks. Get feedback about what steps are missing, how the activities are actually performed in real life, and what descriptions might be more accurate.

- *Brainstorm improvements.* At this point, the lists can be used to start finding areas where things could be stepped up, improved, or completely removed from daily operations. With the goal of being more efficient and more productive, challenge your staff to come up with creative new ideas for ways to do things.

- *Try out new systems.* With the new systems in hand, have your staff try out the new ideas to see if they work or if they still need to be tweaked to be more effective. Try to measure the results to see if you can discern actual improvements.

- *Analyze the results.* Look at the results as the new systems and processes are in place. Find out from staff if the new steps are workable for them or if they still need to have more adjustments.

- *Continue to evaluate your systems.* Go back over your systems routinely to find ways that you can make things better. Sometimes you will need a new piece of technology, and sometimes you will find that newer systems completely replace older activities. The more you can look at where you can improve, the more you will be able to improve.

Though you might have highly effective systems right now, that doesn't mean you can't strive for something better. While you might not make big changes to your systems, even a second of time saved each minute will add up to nearly an hour of saved time each work week.

For most investors, the purchases they make are ones that require them to do as little work as possible once they're purchased. Companies with systems in place for efficiency, human resources, etc., are companies that have more value and that will generate more interest.

Here are some examples of systems you might want to put into place in order to build the confidence of investors:

- *Document templates.* These templates might include everything from checklists to marketing strategies, to schedules and other necessary daily correspondence. The more of these templates you have, the less a new person has to come in and develop new documents to use.
- *Employee handbook.* Since no investor wants to come in and start over completely, having a detailed employee handbook can add value. This handbook should include not only the policies and procedures of the company but also the information about what is expected of every employee. If the rules don't change, then the employees will have an easier transition time, and they will have a better time adapting to rules when they do change.
- *Training procedures.* The more detailed you can be in the way you train your employees, the more investors will be able to see how they will also facilitate those sessions. You will want

to include the different levels of training, what the trainee is expected to learn, and how the training sessions can be adapted for different team members. These training procedures should also include ways in which the sessions might involve testing or feedback to ensure effective outcomes.

- *Process instructions.* When you outline every single process in the company step-by step, it allows anyone to step into that role without needing to ask any questions. They know what to do, and they can just do it. While there is still training that needs to happen, for a new person, these can be invaluable resources when they forget what happens next.

- *Billing procedures.* The more you automate your processes, the more easily someone else can come in and take them over. Since investors may have little to no experience in your industry, they need to be able to see what has already been successful, follow the instructions, and then later find ways to improve upon them (if needed).

- *Job descriptions.* When you have multiple team members, you should have clearly outlined job descriptions for each of them. If they haven't been updated in a while, sit down with each of your employees to find out where things need to be changed and where things need to be removed entirely.

- *Opening/closing procedures.* In companies where there are distinct shifts, having an opening and closing checklist can be helpful for those who are moving between shifts or who are managing teams on these shifts.

- *Ordering/inventory procedures.* Most companies will have a set schedule for their orders and their inventory counts. You may want to include the schedule for these processes, as well as the inventory sheets or software instructions for the next business owner.

- *Trusted/preferred vendors.* In support of the ordering procedure information, having a clear list of the accepted and used vendors helps to ensure the customers still receive the products they expect, as well as the quality.

- *Quality control*. Create a list of the ways in which the quality of the products/services is checked, reviewed, analyzed, and corrected.
- *Work, health, and safety*. A company will want to have a list of the work, health, and safety guidelines that employees are to follow and managers are to implement (even when there is a new owner).
- *Environment and sustainability*. If you have certain ways in which you handle your environmental impact and the sustainability of your business, having a list of these guidelines/procedures/rules will be vital to the company's long-term development.

The more you can put into a binder of information for your company, the more a person who knows nothing about your company can learn and understand the day-to-day activities. This will make your company seem organized (because it is), and it will help the company begin to show how it will provide an easy transition for the next owner.

STEP 8: GET YOURSELF OUT OF THE WAY

Though it might seem that when preparing for a new owner, you should be present in all the processes of the company, this may not be the best plan. Think about how a home is prepared for a seller. Buyers are most interested in homes that contain as little furniture as possible. This allows the person walking into the house to see the potential of the house instead of what the previous owners had for décor.

When a house contains clutter and pictures of the current owners, prospective tenants can have trouble picturing themselves moving in.

To help an investor see himself or herself in your position, you need to find ways to make yourself less involved in the everyday activities.

- *Automate processes.* Instead of you taking on numerous tasks, find ways in which you can have others do those tasks or automate those tasks so they are done without anyone having to do them.
- *Focus on strategies for the future.* Spend less time on the everyday activities of the company and more time on strategizing for what may happen in the future. This time will help support the investor when he or she takes over, and it will help the daily team members be the ones that handle the everyday tasks and duties.
- *Have management lead the teams.* While you may be the person who enjoys leading the teams, ideally, you should step away from this direct leadership when you're in the process of selling. You need to have your team focus on doing what they can do and have you become the person that might guide them but who doesn't interfere with their activities (unless needed).
- *Don't make the final decisions.* Even though you might be the person who used to make all the decisions for the company, that doesn't mean you have to continue to do this. After all, if you're the only person that can make big decisions, what does that mean for your team and their ability to make decisions? A business that depends on you is not a business that will be appealing to an investor.

At the same time, this does not give you license to simply sit around in your office and do nothing. Instead, look at your team and see how they might need support in becoming self-sufficient. That is where your energy should be directed and focused. In doing so, you ensure your company will be able to run itself, even if the new manager or owner doesn't know what to do at first.

STEP 9: CONTINUE TO WORK

Though it's true that you want to find ways to make yourself less important to the daily activities of the company, this doesn't mean you should stop working altogether. Instead, you will need to focus on ways in which you can make the company run even more smoothly.

- *Create exciting promotions.* Perhaps there are ways right now to help promote your company to your existing audience and to new customers. Start implementing new campaigns to attract attention to your business and to manage your brand's identity in the market.
- *Focus on sales boosts.* The more you can boost sales, the better. You need to make sure that you are showing significant sales increases at all times, which will attract the attention of a buyer. In addition, these sales increases will enhance the morale of your team, which will encourage them to be even more effective, which will increase your sales.
- *Bring in new talent/promote team members.* If it makes sense as a part of your company growth strategy, start hiring or promoting talented people. These actions will increase the energy of your company, and you will see other team members perform better.
- *Streamline systems.* While you're readying yourself for offers for your company, look at all the systems you have in your business. Look at each step and try to find ways to make things even more efficient and more productive. The more you can make the company better, the more you will show that your company has potential.

You are still the one in control at this point of your exit plan, and that means you can do a lot in order to increase the appeal of your company. The more you do now, the more results you will see.

Even if you don't plan on being at your company for a longer period of time (at this point), know that the more energy you put into your business, the more you will reap in a sale.

STEP 10: GET YOUR AFFAIRS SETTLED

While you may have worked on all your information to put in a binder for the next person who takes over the company, you also want to make sure you don't leave anything hanging around for them to fix or to find after you are gone.

- *Check your leases.* Since many leases are often on payment schedules, you may not think about them until you get a notice that you need to do something about them. When you're in the process of trying to find a buyer for your company, you need to find out where your leases are at, what you need to do, and whether you are going to renew them.
- *Look at your accounts.* In fact, take some time to look at all the accounts you have in the name of your business. When you do, you will begin to see where you may need to make corrections or where you need to seek additional support to clear things up for a set of new eyes. Seek a professional bookkeeper or accountant to look at the company's books.
- *Renew licenses.* If you have licenses associated with your business, look into their renewal dates and whether or not they can be renewed early. The less work a new owner has to do, the less he or she has to worry about.
- *Look at your staff's training.* Update your staff on the procedures of your company and make sure they are current on HR policies and procedures.
- *Check business insurances.* Make sure to review all the insurance policies associated with your business to ensure they are paid and that the policies are current.

The goal is to make sure you haven't left anything surprising for the new investor to manage or handle. Try to think about all the tasks you accomplish in a year and what you need to pay, settle, or renew. Talk to others who help you complete these tasks, and see if you can create a list of your responsibilities. Then, you can use that list as a checklist to ensure you are getting things done—and on time.

STEP 11: UPDATE YOUR BUSINESS

Even though your business might seem like it's modern and up to date, this will not always be the case. Just as with everything in this world, things change and your business and its customers will change. Because this is something that is consistent, you need to prepare for change now.

It's impossible to find out what will happen in the future. There are no certainties and no trends you can count on. But there are ways you can update your company now. In doing so, all the transitions of the future will be easier and smoother.

Plus, you will encourage buyers to look at your company as an investment in the future.

How Do You Update Your Company?
As you're running the everyday affairs of your company, you notice what works and what doesn't work as well. Some of this is just a temporary change in effectiveness while other changes are indicative of structural problems in the company.

To update your company, you need to ask these questions:

- *What does the market want?* If your business is a success right now, you know what the market is like right now. It can help to make a list of the things the market wants right now in this particular year, and then even look back to see if you can remember what the market wanted before this particular year.

- *Where is the market heading?* With the information about the present and the future, you may be able to see where your company might be headed next. In seeing this information, you can write down some logical predictions. Or you can talk to a business coach or consultant to see if they have any knowledge of your market and where it might be heading.

- *What technology solutions are there?* Though many companies are not technology based and do not work with technical products, you still need to have the most current technical solutions in your company. If you do not, you might seem as though you are out of date and out of touch with reality. Look at what is popular in your industry and whether you are keeping up with everyone else.

- *What is your competition doing?* You may not be able to see everything your competition is doing for its customers, but you should be able to look at their basic technology if you act as though you are a client or a customer. See what they use and how they interact, and then find ways to keep up with them. Of course, you might be the strongest competitor in your field, so if you're the one with the latest technology, stay ahead.

- *What can you afford?* In truth, you might want to have all the fanciest technical solutions and software, but if you can't afford it, you may need to wait a bit. Think about the budget you have available. When you've done that, stop and make a list of the things you want to bring into your company, as well as how you will pay for them.

- *What makes sense for the next ten years?* Looking ahead is something you've already done as a business owner, and it's even more important now that you're exit planning. What is going to be important for your company in the next decade? Where do you think things are headed?

A lot of times in this book, you've been asked to think about what your market is doing and how you think your market will respond in the future. If you're not sure how to answer these questions, it might be helpful to follow this advice:

- *Set up Google Alerts*. There is a free tool on Google that can help you collect information about keywords as they relate to your market and to your company in particular. Just pick some words and phrases and enter them into this system. You will get regular updates about information that's related online. With this information, you can decide what you need to do or what needs to happen in the future.
- *Look for customer reviews*. You need to have an ear open for the comments of the people who are buying your products. If you don't know what they want and what they need from you, you can't deliver. Make sure you read all the reviews, good and bad, to find out what the market may need and how it might be shifting in certain ways.
- *Research the online marketplace*. Look at your industry and your marketplace as though you were a customer. Look at all the websites out there. Look at all the informational sites as well as the shopping sites. See what customers see when they go out to shop. Find out if you would be excited by the available options. See if you notice anything that's missing. Find out what the marketplace is doing for customers, and see if you can do it better.
- *Consider website trends*. It's not just about looking at websites in your industry either. Look at as many websites as you can to see what the website design strategies might be. See if your

website is keeping up with the times or if you need to make updates.

- *Visit related forums.* Since people use the Internet to talk, there are forums of every kind available. On these forums, people will talk about their lives, the products they use, and the websites they visit. By visiting these forums, you can hear what real customers are saying about your company and about what you have to offer next. You can even ask questions of the people on the forums to see if you can understand their thinking about their purchases.
- *Bring in a marketing strategist.* While the idea of another professional in your life might seem overwhelming, bringing in someone who understands trends and how they emerge can be beneficial. This person can give you an overall assessment of your company and how it needs to be updated to maintain its relevance in the market.

The more you look at your company, the more you will begin to see how/where/why it needs to be updated. But you have to look carefully so you don't miss something your customers have already noticed.

STEP 12: IMPROVE YOUR TALENT

In your company, you have a team that completes the tasks of the day and helps build stronger results. This talented team may not be large, but they are the people who continuously ensure that your customers and clients come back.

Your talent includes:

- *Management.* You might have a management team that works on the larger picture and the strategic direction of your company. This might just include you if you have a smaller company, or it might include a group of supervisors, managers, etc.

- *Staff.* The core of your talent is your daily staff. While they might have a variety of titles, they are assigned and perform the tasks that keep your company up and running. The more they do, the more results your company sees.

- *Contractors.* You might also employ contractors, or people who are not actual employees. These are the people you hire for certain projects and who are called on to support in special circumstances. Some companies primarily use contractors, as they do not receive benefits or other special employee advantages.

- *Professional advisers.* In addition, you might have professional advisers on your team who help you make the bigger decisions for the company. Though they might not be on staff, they are still a crucial part of your talent.

You may have hired all these individuals, they might be a part of your family, or they might be people who were already on board when you arrived as an owner. No matter who they are and what they provide for your company, they are the talent that sustains you. To ensure your company is ready for any type of future, you need to be confident in your team.

WHO TO KEEP

Every business needs to make decisions when it comes to their team. While some companies are actively trying to save money, others are looking for ways to make their team stronger. As a business owner who wants to sell your company, your team is just as valuable (if not more valuable) as the products you sell.

But you want to keep only the team members who add to your bottom line. Here are specifics to look at when making the tough decisions about who to keep as a part of your staff:

- *Years at the company*. Though someone who has worked at a company for a long time doesn't necessarily have talent, loyalty can also be a valuable asset for an investor. It can help to keep on the people who have been around longer, as they know the systems of the company better than anyone else and can adjust more easily to change.

- *Knowledge and skill set*. You also want to look at the skills and knowledge of each person on your team. Find out what they can do, what they like to do, and what they are learning to do. The more a person knows, the more he or she can contribute to the company's overall success.

- *Expertise level*. Measuring expertise can be a little trickier. For many companies, this measurement is a combination of years working in the field, training, and hands-on experience. Some measure this based on how much training a person has had. But even then, a person can be skilled in something they have no training in, so that may not work in all cases.

- *Ability to collaborate*. Teams should be able and willing to work with one another. Note too that collaboration and teamwork are not always one and the same. You can work on a team with someone else and not collaborate. A talented team member is someone who can work with others *and* share ideas and insights, listen to input and feedback, and support the activities of the team. A person who is more than just someone who punches the clock and does his or her work is an asset in your organization.

- *Accomplishments/achievements*. It's time to think about what each person has done for you at your company. While anyone can work on everyday tasks and get the basics done, not everyone can achieve results. Consider all the things your team has contributed and accomplished, and make your team decisions based on those results.

When you're trying to make decisions about who to hire and whom the team should include, be sure to include the people you are evaluating. It can help to sit down in the office with them and see what they think about their performance and future.

Talk to them about why they feel their role is essential in the company and what they bring that no one else does. Even if they're not sure how to answer that question, the way they try to answer the question can help you better understand what you need to do to arrange your team in the best way possible.

HOW TO IMPROVE

As you continue looking at your team to see what needs to change and how you need to improve your organization, consider how you can develop the team you have. While it might seem easier to choose new people to fill in the gaps in your team, there are many benefits to working with the people you have right now.

- *Lower training costs.* When you're looking at your costs and how you can maximize your budget, you will want to focus on training who you already have in your company rather than training someone who has never worked for you. If you train a current employee, it won't take as long, and it won't be added time in their day (or on their paycheck). But when you train someone without any experience, he or she will need more training time, more time to adapt to what he or she has learned, and more time to find out how to work well in the new setting. This all adds up to more labor costs and the possibility of not necessarily getting an employee who will stay in the long term.

- *Less risk*. If you're training a new employee, there is always the chance that you might not have this employee around for a long time. True, new employees might stay with the company for a bit, but there's a risk they will simply move on when they find something new. This can disrupt your operations, and it can make other team members less pleased with the team dynamics. Though it's true that you also take a risk on anyone who is on your team, new and untested employees are often more of a challenge.

- *Morale improvement*. A company that actively seeks to develop its own employees is a company where employees feel valued and appreciated. They know they will get the support they need to learn a task, and they know they will be given more knowledge so they can do their job well. This helps everyone feel as though they are a part of something special, which makes them work even harder to succeed.

- *More loyalty*. Employees who know their management is focused on making them the best possible employees are more likely to stay with their company. With a consistent team and a team who is willing to be loyal, the entire company benefits.

Once you have decided who you want to keep, there are several ways in which you can develop their skills and build their talent in the organization:

- *Training*. The first thing you will want to do when you are developing your team is to work on training them in the skills they already have or the ones they need to cultivate. This training might look like going over old training, or it might look like working on reviewing new training pieces they may not have experienced. Though some team members may not like having to go through training again, when everyone is doing what the training manual says, the team will be more effective, consistent, and productive (assuming you have updated your training and procedures).

- *Outside training.* In addition, it can help to encourage your team to find outside training that will benefit their current job roles. You might be able to pay for this training, or you might allow the employee the time away to complete this training on his or her own. When you support additional learning, employees will grow in their ability to support the company, and they will grow in their understanding of how their actions benefit the whole of the organization.

- *Support for further education.* When you can support your employees in higher education and training, you give them the tools they need to perform well, but you also help them in their larger career goals. While you might want them to stay at your company forever, this is not always possible or realistic. Instead, you might support educational goals (via helping with payments or time off) if the employees stay with the company for a certain number of years. This will encourage learning as well as loyalty.

- *Mentoring roles.* An employee who is partnered up with a more experienced member of the company will be able to learn from the mentor. This doesn't have to be a training relationship but rather a person to check in with in order to learn more about how to be a better part of the company. Each person can learn from the other, and this can also set up a simple succession program when the more senior team member decides to leave the company or retire.

- *Trainer positions.* It's also helpful for each team member to act as a trainer for others in the company. Though they may not always be the trainer, they might be the person who will step into a training role when needed. When people train someone else, they often see where they might improve their own skills, and they become even more valuable.

As a business owner, you need to be ready to develop your team members, as they are the most valuable parts of your company. You can ascertain when you need to build more training into your company culture by doing the following:

- *Have regular performance reviews.* As a leader, it's imperative that you review the performance of the team you have hired and trained. This will help them understand how they are succeeding and where they need to improve their skills. In addition, you can offer concrete ways for the team to improve, allowing them to show how they have grown in the time between reviews. (Plus, this is a great time to show that pay increases are the reward for hard work.)
- *Give specific feedback.* You don't have to wait for reviews to give a team member feedback. In fact, it's often more effective to give a team member feedback when something isn't going right. In the moment, a correction can make more sense and be heard by the team member. Be specific in what isn't correct and why it isn't correct, and then offer a solution. Check back in with team members later to see if they have noticed their work change since instituting the feedback. Positive feedback is also appreciated and very effective in boosting staff morale.
- *Encourage team members to give advice to one another.* You can't be everywhere all the time, so it's a good practice to have the entire team work together on feedback. Each person can offer feedback, helping to build the overall strength of the team as well as ensuring positive communication. To ensure feedback is given effectively, the team should learn how to give constructive feedback—by being specific, being timely, and being focused on the activity and not on the person.

The more you build your team, the more your business will grow. But even with all this advice, you might find yourself in a situation where you need to hire someone from outside, which means you will need to approach your training and development slightly differently.

- *Screen your applicants well*. Even with the best training plan, if you're not choosing the best possible employees, you will not have the results you want. The best thing to do is to make sure you're hiring only the best possible people for the jobs. Make sure you have a strong understanding of what you want to see in an employee and what you want to build in terms of a team.
- *Have a trial period*. It can be helpful to have a clearly defined training period that both you and the employee are aware of. This will help employees see that they can change their mind about the job and choose to leave. You, too, can make up your mind about an employee. You may decide to let them go if you don't see progress, for example.
- *Use a strong trainer*. Though it might be easier to just have anyone train new employees, the goal is to make sure they're trained as well as possible the first time. When this is your goal, putting the best possible trainer in place is essential. You want new employees to feel they are getting the support as well as the information they need to succeed. A training checklist can be helpful to ensure all important topics are covered, and it allows for consistency.
- *Test knowledge*. During various parts of the training, it's a good idea to test the knowledge of trainees. Find out what they know, what they still don't know, etc. The more they are tested, the more you can see if they are taking the training seriously or if they are not the right person for the job.
- *Put the trainee into real situations as soon as possible*. To see how the training is working, or not, for employees, get them into a real-life scenario (i.e., meeting with a customer, taking

an order, etc.). This will show how the training is going, and it will also help you see if new employees are working out and if they need to be let go before they take up more labor costs.

- *Give immediate feedback and corrections.* While training should be a time to make trainees feel welcome, it is also a time when they should be given direct feedback and corrections. When they get this information, they can change their actions before they become habits that are hard to break.
- *Ask trainers about the progress of the trainee.* During the training process, the trainers should be carefully questioned about their trainees. Listen to their feedback and see if there are any signals that the new trainee may not be the best fit for the company.

Now, much of this information can also be applied to training existing employees as well. The more dedicated the training process is, the more effective it will be.

The team you create will be the team that makes an investor want your company even more.

STEP 13: SET UP A BUSINESS PLAN

In the continuing spirit of helping an investor see the value of your company, creating or refining your business plan becomes the next natural step.

Most companies created this plan when they first started out or when they needed to get a business loan for starting their everyday operations. But others may not have created a business plan or may not have updated it for some time.

No matter where you are in this situation, it's time to set up a business plan that will increase the confidence of the prospective buyer and help you stay organized in your operations.

WHAT A BUSINESS PLAN DOES

A business plan is used to define the structure of a company and to help others who might be evaluating the company see its potential. Other benefits/uses of a business plan include:

- *It provides a clear direction.* When you create a business plan, you outline the ways in which your business will operate and how it will manage its everyday tasks. Though you might not include every single detail of every single task, when you want to bring in new investors or a new owner, you will want to be as detailed as you can.
- *It provides an overall strategy.* Many business plans include a mission statement or something similar. While this might seem like a silly thing, it actually helps bring the company back to its roots and its goals. If you're ever in a position where you're not sure what to do, you can review the mission statement and make your decision based on whether or not the choice serves the bigger picture.
- *It provides a financial picture.* The business plan will also have the financial details of your company, including a forecast for the next five or ten years. Having this information, a reader can see what the expected growth is and what the current assets and expenses are.
- *It provides a human resources structure.* You can also include a clear outline of the staff structure and its members at the present time. In addition, some companies find it helpful to include their organizational development strategies (hiring, firing, recruiting, etc.).

- *It provides a succession strategy.* For some business plans with managers who plan to retire at certain ages, it can also include information about what the succession plan looks like and who will take their places.
- *It provides a plan for company growth.* If you have a business plan, it can be used as a way to see what has worked in the past, and it can serve as a jumping-off point for what might happen in the future. The business plan is not a static object, nor should it be something that is rigid. It should be reviewed every few years to see what stays, what goes, and what shifts to serve new goals.
- *It provides an investor report/proposal.* Of course, while you already may have used a business plan to get money from a bank, you can also use it to entice investors to buy your company.

The business plan should be a document you spend time and energy creating. Though it might not seem like something you will look at every day, you may find it becomes more valuable when you need to show the appeal of your company to someone outside of your daily operations.

THE PARTS OF A TYPICAL BUSINESS PLAN

While there are certainly parts of a business plan that are expected, you may also want to do some research into what else you could put into your plan, since you are crafting the plan for the growth that will happen after you are gone.

When you're trying to write up a business plan, it can help to include the basic tenets:

- *Mission statement and/or vision statement.* This is the guiding principle that will drive the movement of your company and its decisions. You will want to make this a unique and specific statement about what your company can do and what it wants to do within its target market.

- *Description of your company and product or service.* Simply put, this is the summary of what your company does and what it will sell to its audience. Again, you want to be as specific as possible here, helping to inform the reader about what your company does (and also what your company does that other companies do not).

- *Your unique selling proposition (USP).* To be more specific, you will want to describe exactly what you have to offer that sets you apart from others. What makes you unique, and what makes you the company that a customer would choose above all others?

- *Market analysis.* Just as you will look at your market to see how you fit in, you want to provide the reader with an idea of what the market already includes, what you bring, etc. The more you can show that you have considered the market, the more you will be able to show how the company can succeed in the market. In this section, it's best to talk about the competition, how your company has fared in relation to the competition, etc. It is also important to explain why the competition has fared the way it has and what your company did to impact the competition's performance.

- *Marketing strategy.* When you have outlined what the market wants from you and what it looks like, you can begin to describe how you will meet the market's needs. You need to talk about your key messages and where you will be marketing (i.e., social media, billboards, direct mail, etc.). By considering the best ways to reach your audience, you will make sure you show the investor you are doing all you can to increase your sales and profits.

- *SWOT analysis.* The more you analyze your company, the more an investor will be able to see what the benefits/downsides of buying your company will be. SWOT represents strengths, weaknesses, opportunities, and threats.
  - *Strengths.* These are the points of your company that have been seen as strengths in relation to the overall operational structure. These might include your USP, your strategies, etc.
  - *Weaknesses.* Every company has some weaknesses, and it can help to outline these in detail. At the same time, when you see these weaknesses, you can take some time to correct them before you start the process of selling your company (or you can show you're in the process of correcting the issues).
  - *Opportunities.* You might want to showcase how you see the company doing more in the future and how the company is positioned for greater growth and brand positioning in the coming years.
  - *Threats.* It also helps to show the threats you can see in the market and the possible challenges in the future.
- *Revenue projections.* In this part of the business plan, you outline the revenue you estimate you will make in the coming years. Though this is certainly an estimate of your success, it is based on how you have fared in the past.
- *Cash flow statement.* This statement demonstrates how changes in balance sheet accounts and income impact the cash and cash equivalents. You can break up this analysis into operating, investing, and financing activity totals.
- *Summary/conclusion.* At the end, you can summarize all the information in the business plan, effectively selling the company to a potential investor.

Writing the business plan should be a process in which you consider all the information about your business and you show how things are supposed to work. While this plan can be a starting point in a conversation with a buyer, it's also a great tool for seeing how your company is working—and how it could work better.

STEP 14: QUALIFY PROSPECTIVE BUYERS

While you might be eager to sell, you don't want to simply choose anyone to be the buyer of your company. After all, you've worked hard to get where you are, and you don't want to hand the keys over to anyone who might have a large check to offer to you. Instead, you need to qualify the buyers at your door.

You need to make the purchase of your business more than just a transaction. In showing you aren't just looking for any person, you will encourage those who are serious and those who are going to see the value of your company to seek you out.

- *Have a list of desirable traits.* The best way to make sure you get the right buyer for your company is to describe the person you want at the helm. This means you need to think about more than just the payment you want to receive; you also want to think about the quality of the bidder. Think about who this person is, what he or she brings to the company, why he or she is interested, what he or she has to offer, what he or she has to add, etc.
- *Seek out prospective bidders.* Though you might hear that most bidders are going to come to you, this isn't always the case. Instead, you might need to seek out the bidders who will take over your company. Find people in your area who have already shown an interest in you and in companies like yours. The more you reach out, the more word will get around that you are

interested in selling. Reaching out can be done through your network, approaching your competition or organizations that could benefit from your products and services. Seeking out bidders is normally an activity a business broker will perform or can assist you with.

- *Pitch your company.* When finding prospective investors, meet with them and sell the company's benefits and attributes. You will begin to see what makes people interested in your company and what makes them nervous. Even if you don't end up finding a buyer this way, you will collect information, which will make your company more viable and more likely to be purchased. A business broker can assist with the initial pitching of your company, but any prospective investor will want to hear the story of the business from the owner. The passion an owner has for his or her business is often what sparks the interest in investors and gets them over the line.

The more you can show that you won't just sell to anyone, the more you will attract the right buyers to your company. Since you're probably not in the position where you want to sell instantly, you have the luxury of time and selectiveness.

If you are looking to sell more quickly, it might be that you will take a lower price than you may have at another time in your career, but that still doesn't mean you should settle for just any buyer.

RESOURCES

Below are some checklists to help you increase the value of your company.

INCREASING BUSINESS VALUE—FOURTEEN VALUE ENHANCERS

In what level of detail have you considered the following as part of increasing the value of your company?	1 = Not Good 5 = Good
1. Make your business attractive. - Finding out what your company looks like in the market. - Seeking out criticism. - Increasing brand positioning. - Starting community outreach. - Sharing your company's successes.	
2. Increase your profits. - Finding out what your customers want. - Meeting the needs of loyal customers. - Seeking out new customers/identify new markets. - Improving your marketing strategy. - Adding recurring items. - Adopting the 3X financial model.	
3. Document the things people can't see. - Proprietary research and formulas. - How you acquire new customers. - How you evaluate locations. - How you satisfy a customer. - How you approach product strategies.	
4. Clear your debts. - Find out what your debts are. - Talk with vendors. - Create payment plans. - Reduce extras. - Eliminate unnecessary staff. - Focus on debt payments.	
5. Promote your positive cash flow. - Show the numbers. - Reveal your strategy. - Explain times when things are not positive.	

In what level of detail have you considered the following as part of increasing the value of your company?	1 = Not Good 5 = Good
6. Organize your books.	
- Hire a professional.	
- Find your receipts.	
- Determine the best categories.	
- Review the results.	
- Listen to recommendations.	
- Get a second opinion.	
- Separate family and business expenses.	
7. Create systems.	
- List all your processes.	
- Write out all the steps.	
- Ask for staff feedback and adjustments.	
- Brainstorm improvements.	
- Try out new systems.	
- Analyze the results.	
- Continue to evaluate your systems.	
8. Get yourself out of the way.	
- Automate processes.	
- Focus on strategies for the future.	
- Have management lead the teams.	
- Don't make the final decisions.	
9. Continue to work.	
- Create exciting promotions.	
- Focus on sales boosts.	
- Bring in new talent/promote team members.	
- Streamline systems.	
10. Get your affairs settled.	
- Check your leases.	
- Look at your accounts.	
- Renew licenses.	
- Look at your staff's training.	
- Check business insurances.	

In what level of detail have you considered the following as part of increasing the value of your company?	1 = Not Good 5 = Good
11. Update your business. - What does the market want? - Where is the market heading? - What technology solutions are there? - What is your competition doing? - What can you afford? - What makes sense for the next ten years?	
12. Improve your talent. - Management; staff; contractors; professional advisers. - Who to keep. - How to improve.	
13. Set up a business plan. - A clear direction. - An overall strategy. - A financial picture. - A human resources structure. - A succession strategy. - A plan for company growth. - An investor report/proposal.	
14. Qualify prospective buyers. - Have a list of desirable traits. - Seek out prospective bidders. - Pitch your company.	

BUSINESS PLAN

Does your business plan cover the following in enough detail to be effective?	1 = Not Good 5 = Good
Mission statement and/or vision statement	
Description of your company and products and services	
Your unique selling proposition (USP)	
Market analysis	

Does your business plan cover the following in enough detail to be effective?	1 = Not Good 5 = Good
Marketing strategy	
SWOT analysis	
Revenue projections	
Cash flow statement	

MONEY MATTERS

You can be young without money, but
you can't be old without it.

—Tennessee Williams

In this chapter, we talk about what retirement planning, insurance, estate planning, and tax planning look like. While working with professionals in these areas will help you customize your approach to planning, the more you know about these money matters, the more you will be ready to manage them. And even if you're not around to manage these issues, you can have things in place so that your family doesn't have to worry about them.

While it might seem strange to wait until now to talk about money, your financial situation is often greatly impacted by the sale of your business. In fact, everything works hand in hand, as you are not necessarily going to quit your job tomorrow or hand over the keys to your company at the end of the day.

Ideally, you have time to consider all the things you need to do in order to prepare for a new way of living—outside of the office. The way you set up your money and your finances matters more than you might realize.

Even though you may be completely aware that you need money in order to survive, it's not always clear how much money you might need to make things comfortable for you and for your family.

RETIREMENT PLANNING

When you go to sell your company, you may not have thought about the fact that you were setting yourself up for retirement. It might just seem like another business transaction rather than the actual shutdown of your company (at least for you as the owner).

As such, some business owners forget to plan for their retirement. And to be truthful, many small-business owners believe they will be in their companies forever, so they have no plan at all for the future. They simply hope they will have enough.

You need to do better than that. Ideally, you will have sold your company for a good portion of money, but if you have not, then you will need to have additional funding available.

But how much?

HOW MUCH INCOME DO YOU NEED?

The first thing you need to do in order to plan for your retirement is to find out what you will need to pay once you're no longer working. You need to consider the lifestyle you want, charities, money you will need to pay the government, and money you will need to support your family.

Start by looking at everything you pay now:

- mortgage/rent
- utilities
- insurance
- food
- clothing
- entertainment
- car/motorcycle/transportation
- health care
- taxes
- debts

- gifts
- tithes and offerings
- education
- savings and investments
- special events and purchases
- miscellaneous (i.e., gyms, hobbies, etc.)
- vacations you want to take

This list might be longer for you, so take time to think about what you have to pay for each month. Go through your bank account to see what bills you pay and what you will still need to pay when you are no longer working.

If you're not planning on exiting your business for a while, you may have fewer expenses than this list contains, as you may pay off your house or your car, decreasing your overall expenses.

But this process doesn't end with finding out how much you need to pay each month. You need to then consider when you want to retire. Now, after seeing your expenses, you might find your original desired retirement date needs to be pushed back in order to ensure you have the money you need.

At the same time, if you decide you want to retire on a certain date in a certain year, this number might help to motivate you to build up those retirement funds more quickly.

While you can't necessarily know how long you will live, another factor in retirement planning is your life expectancy. The longer you live, the more money you will need.

In addition, if you are paying for any of your family's expenses (and you wish to continue to do so), you will need to add that to your overall expenses.

With this information, you will see how much money you anticipate spending until you die.

It is better to estimate more than less, so be sure to add up items and account for emergencies and other unintended expenses.

The more money you have available at this time, the better for everyone who is counting on it.

WHAT DO YOU HAVE?

Next, you need to consider if there are any additional income sources you will have after you leave your business. Some owners will have a passive income stream from their companies, without having to go into the office anymore. This can be in the form of retaining some interest in the business after you exit, having your successor run the business, or as a result of an earn-out arrangement during the sale. Earn-out is discussed in more detail in the next section.

Others will seek out new jobs, or their spouses/partners will have income to be put toward expenses.

If you're not sure if you will have income or you're not sure of its reliability, it's best to simply not factor it into the conversation about how much money you will have waiting for you when you retire.

You may also have income from investments or savings accounts that can help to offset the amount of money you will need to spend during your retirement years.

Like the expenses you already calculated, it's ideal that you adjust the rate of income. But in this case, you want to estimate that you will bring in less money. This will help you to be prepared in any situation, and it will allow you to be able to continue to live comfortably.

Other income streams might include:

- insurance payouts/superannuation/pension
- gifts
- shares

Again, if you're not sure of the income you might be able to receive after you have retired, then do not count these amounts toward your overall funds available.

Instead, plan to have less, and then you'll be surprised when you have more.

BUSINESS EARN-OUT

It has become more prevalent when selling a business for there to be some form of earn-out as part of the sales price. In calculating what you have, you need to take into account that the sale of your business could have an earn-out attached to it.

What is an earn-out? It is a mechanism where the purchase price is fully or (more often) partially calculated by using the future performance of the business. A common way of calculating this is by reference to profits over, for example, the two or three financial periods after the sale. It is also possible, but less usual, to link the earn-out to sales or any other financial measure that might be appropriate to the sale.

Earn-outs have advantages to the buyer and you. For you, the advantages are:

- It may provide a way for you to reap the full benefit of selling a profitable business. Without an earn-out, the price the buyer is prepared to pay may be discounted as a result of doubt about the actual profitability of your business.
- It may give you an opportunity to benefit from the advantages of being part of a larger buyers' group. However, it can also give rise to a number of difficult issues in the process.

The advantages for the buyer are:

- It ensures that part of the purchase price is directly linked to the actual performance of your business after the sale. This can remove a significant element of uncertainty from the sale and result in a better price being offered.
- Part of the purchase price will be deferred for a period after sale, which is beneficial from a cash flow perspective.
- In a scenario where you are considered key to the business, the existence of an earn-out can be seen as an incentive to you to retain your loyalty in the business after the sale. This is the case where the buyer would ask you to remain in the business for a period after the sale.

Disadvantages of an earn-out are:

- You might want to have a clean break on completion of the sale. An earn-out means that you will retain a very significant interest and, in most cases, a day-to-day involvement in the business going forward.
- At the most general level, both you and the buyer have an interest in maximizing profits after completion. However, a significant number of issues are likely to arise in the negotiation of the earn-out, which can give rise to conflict between the two sides.

- Fluctuations in profitability in the period after the sale can make it extremely difficult to exclude such fluctuations from the earn-out calculation. This may work to the advantage or disadvantage of either party, depending on the circumstances.
- Earn-outs can (and very often do) give rise to particularly tricky and complex taxation questions, which require specialist input and a good working knowledge of the tax issues that can be faced.

An earn-out should be carefully considered, and you should seek the advice of your professional team before agreeing to an earn-out as part of the sale of your business.

INVESTMENT RISK

Before we look at the gap that might exist between the funds you need and the funds you have for your retirement and how investments can help you fill the gap, it's important to get a picture in your mind of the level of investment risk you are willing to take.

Investment risk is the chance that an investment's actual return will be different from what you expected. Risk includes the possibility of losing some or all your original investment.

With the economy and markets moving up and down like a roller coaster, it's important that you carefully consider the various risks that are associated with each investment you make. The fact is, many people have no knowledge about how to protect themselves from unneeded risk.

Whether it is investing, driving, or just walking down the street, everyone exposes themselves to risk. Your personality and lifestyle play a big role in how much risk you are comfortably able to take on.

If you invest in stocks and have trouble sleeping at night, you are probably taking on too much risk.

When investing in stocks, bonds, or any investment instrument, there is a lot more risk than you might think. Some of the risk to consider includes foreign exchange rates, interest rates, the market, politics, etc.

The risk-return trade-off could easily be called the iron stomach test. Deciding what amount of risk you can take on is one of the most important investment decisions you will make.

The risk-return tradeoff is the balance you must decide on between the desires for the lowest possible risk for the highest possible returns. Remember to keep in mind that low levels of uncertainty (low risk) are associated with low potential returns, and high levels of uncertainty (high risk) are associated with high potential returns.

With the stock markets bouncing up and down 5 percent every week, as an investor you clearly need a safety net. Diversification of your investments can work this way and can prevent your entire investment portfolio from losing value.

Different individuals will have different tolerances for risk. Tolerance is not static; it will change as your life does. As you grow older, tolerance will usually shrink as more and more obligations come up, including retirement.

Managing the risk of your investments can be complex, and seeking the advice of a financial planner to help you identify and manage your investment risk is worth the investment.

MINDING THE GAP

For most business owners, their business value contributes the largest part of their wealth.

Often business owners perceive the value of their business to be much higher than it is, leaving a gap the day they sell their business. It is important to be realistic about the price you will get for your business.

The key to effective retirement planning is understanding the gap between what you need and what you have. The more you can define and clarify what this gap might be, the more you can prepare for your future.

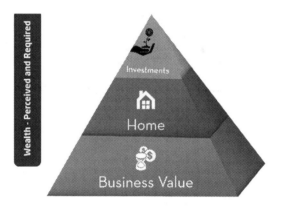

You need to understand where you are at and what you need so that you can retire at an age and time when it will make sense and when you will be able to live without worry about your finances.

The money will need to be accessible, and it should be able to sustain you for the years that you and your family have left together.

Some sources of this funding will be:

Savings
The most common place to find the funding you have for the future is your savings accounts. You might choose to set these up in your bank, or you might have another place for your funds to be safe and secure.

This money might come from setting aside money each month, and it might come from the sale of your part of the business. You might have other funds from other sources (i.e., side income, side project monies, etc.).

The savings you build up does not have to be the bulk of your retirement planning, but it can be limited in a variety of ways.

What you need to remember is that a savings account, even with interest, is still going to be a finite resource. Once you've spent what you have, you will not have the ability to have more—unless you go back to work.

This is why it's important to find a way to put the money you have saved into places where it will work hard for you.

When you continuously make returns on the money you saved, you will be able to have more money and take away less from the overall funds available. Globally, interest rates have been practically nothing since the financial crisis that began in late 2008. So, interest payments are not going to appreciably increase principal or provide retirement cash flow. Even bonds will fail to do so. Consideration should be given to possible investments in dividend-paying blue-chip stocks. Today's current economic environment is a good argument in favor of setting up the sale of your business so payments are gradual, with you sharing in some of the growth, despite the risk that the company might go under with the new management running the business.

On the other hand, some feel that having a savings account with everything they need is the best way to know they have what they need and that they don't have to rely on the market's trends.

You can make this decision for yourself.

Investments (Stock, Property)

The next most common way to prepare for your retirement is to think about the way you might invest in the future. As noted before, investing is something that is often more effective than simply saving up funds, but it's also more complicated for many people who are not sure how to begin and how to maintain an investment portfolio.

Here are some ways to begin the investment process.

- *Hire a professional to help.* Though you might be able to make investments on your own, or you have in the past, it can be more effective to work with a professional. They will be able to give you a plan to meet your investing goals, while also educating you about what investments make sense for your age and for your current budget limitations.
- *Start looking at the markets.* While you might not understand everything you read when it comes to the stock market or real estate market, it's a good idea to think about learning how

things move up and down. Try looking at the markets to see what happens, what the professionals are saying about the trends, and what their advice includes.

- *Educate yourself.* Think about ways you can educate yourself to learn more about how the markets work. You can read books, peruse websites, and try to find information that's relevant to the type of investing you want to do.

- *Start with a low-risk investment.* If you have not invested before, it's ideal that you begin with a small, low-risk investment. This will help you see what the process looks like and how investments work.

- *Invest what you can afford to lose right now.* When you're not already in a strong financial position, the best advice is to make sure you're investing only what you can afford to lose. Since investing can be high risk, you want to use money that is outside of your traditional budget. While there are investments that will have a lower risk, those investments also tend to have lower returns.

- *Invest for the long term.* As you begin to invest, it can be tempting to look at your portfolio over and over to see what is happening. Though this is not a bad idea, the markets can be volatile. As a result, you might notice your investment go way up and then way down. For those who don't have a strong stomach for these types of movements, you may not want to look at your accounts for a while. In addition, it's best to remember that investing is a long-term approach. You want to check your accounts sporadically to see the general trend, not the ongoing changes that are normal and expected.

- *Keep things diverse.* The more you can diversify your investments, the more effective you can be. Diversity means having your money in a number of different places. When you follow this approach, one investment can do badly, but others will not. It's the idea of not having all your eggs in one basket, as you don't want to lose all your eggs before you plan to retire.

What kinds of investments are out there for you to use? Broadly there are three main categories of investments that you can consider:

- *Ownership investments.* These are investments in which you pay money in order to own something (i.e., stocks, real estate, etc.). When you give your money in this situation, you're not just getting something in return, you're also betting that what you purchased will grow in value the longer you own it. While there are certainly situations in which this does not happen, and thus these are considered to be riskier investments, the overall track record for ownership investments is positive.
- *Cash investments.* When you're looking into cash investments, you might go to a bank. These types of investments include bank accounts (savings) and bonds. A safer and more secure investment, these investments will pay out what they have promised to pay out, and they will not lose value. Even if you don't make anything on the investment, you will not lose what you paid into it either.
- *Retirement funds.* The funds could comprise a pension plan where you will receive an agreed monthly payment from a certain age until you die. Other options include superannuation funds that provide tax benefits, but access to funds is limited.

Each of these investment options (and there are others) will help you create a comprehensive strategy for your future. But you need to understand what they are and how they can add to your exit plan.

Investing is a highly complicated part of exit-planning and financial preparation. Many people are able to make investments on their own, but a professional is strongly encouraged.

A professional investment strategist can:

- *Help you set up a long-term plan.* Since these professionals understand how the markets work, they can come up with a long-term plan that is customized to your earning goals and retirement needs. They will also work on plans that can continue to work for you after you have left your company.
- *Give advice about investments to make.* With all the different investments available, it's best for you to be educated by a professional. They will give you the pros and the cons of each option, and they will answer questions you might have.
- *Manage your investments when they reach a certain point.* If you give your investment strategist your parameters for investing, they can make small adjustments to your portfolio without needing to get your permission. This means you don't need to watch your investments at all times.
- *Oversee a larger investment strategy.* The investment professional will be able to craft a larger investment strategy, or portfolio, with a blend of risk and potential rewards. In doing so, he or she can hold the bigger picture and can help you stay calm about the future.
- *Update you when necessary.* Since you may not need to have updates all the time, nor should you need them when your investment strategy is not going to show rewards for a while, the investment strategist can help by updating you on a quarterly basis. He or she will reach out to you only when you need to know something has changed.

Though you might think hiring another professional to manage your money is just going to reduce your overall savings, realize that when you have someone handle your investments for you, they can often help you avoid costly mistakes.

In addition, they may know how to manage the market and its changes, especially when they've been working with the markets in the past few years.

Just let them know your goals and the risk you are willing to take, and they'll get you started on the way to a positive financial future.

Retirement Fund
Retirement funds you contribute to will differ from country to country and generally include one or more of the following:

- 401k
- defined contribution plans
- pension plans
- superannuation funds
- retirement annuity funds

What many people don't realize is that their retirement funds may not be enough. For those who are lucky to have this sort of fund in place, they might take for granted this fund will meet their future needs, as well as keep up with cost of living and with inflation.

But this is far from the case.

If you have a retirement fund, you need to take some time to figure out what it means and how it might help you. In some funds, there are specific amounts that can be drawn at a certain time for a certain time period.

You may have established the rate at which you were going to be given money for your future when you started contributing to the fund. While at the time you signed up for the fund, it might have been the right rate for your expected cost of living and goals, this total may not be the right one for the new plans for your future.

In this case, you want to think about how the gap might be filled.

Even a few years of contributing to these funds can help you get ahead financially. These funds are often tax sheltered, and they can help reduce your income taxes as well since they do not add to your income until you start to draw from them.

THE INSURANCE YOU NEED

Insurance allows you to have an extra layer of protection from the unexpected. Though these bad things may never happen, being ready for them anyway will help protect not only those around you but also your financial health and well-being.

For some, having insurance may be something they don't think about. Some governments (for example, Australia) offer their citizens health coverage as a part of their taxes. But in other cases, a person looking to exit his or her company may need to buy health insurance. Health care costs are handled differently in every country, and you should ensure that you have enough insurance to cover the costs.

Being sick is costly in some areas, after all, and treatments can drain bank accounts for those who are not covered by the right types of insurance.

INSURANCE TYPES

When you're preparing for retirement, look at the insurance you have and the insurance you want to have. Though this may depend on the area in which you live, it's best to consider all the possibilities, as you may not live in the same location for the rest of your life.

Here are the types of insurance you may want to consider in preparation for your exit plan:

- *Health*. In some countries, you may be able to get your health insurance through the plan at your company for a certain amount of time after you leave your position. Or you might be able to write this possibility into the sales documents to ensure you are covered in the case of your eventual move into retirement. For some, this might not be possible, so you will need to look into alternatives. Private policies are available, though they can be expensive, and they can continue to increase in price as you become older.

- *Life*. In the event of your death, you want to have enough money available for your loved ones. A life insurance policy can help to protect your family, but you will need to ensure the amount of coverage will help them effectively. Some people choose to buy a policy that is enough to cover any remaining bills, as well as to ease the transition from having a family member around to not having that member around. In addition, you might want to consider getting a life insurance policy that is big enough to take care of your family in the event that you pass away before your retirement and before some of your long-term financial strategies can come to fruition.

- *Long-term care*. Some areas of the world require payment for long-term care. This includes rehabilitation units, nursing homes, and other facilities that support patients for long periods. You might also include in-home care in this category. Because traditional health insurance policies do not include these services, you need to allot extra in your budget to pay for these services and ensure your family doesn't have to struggle to pay for the care you or someone else in your family might need.

- *Disability/income protection/permanent disability.* If you were to become disabled or injured in some way, you might not be able to work, or you might not be able to do things as you would have liked. By having disability insurance, income protection insurance, and permanent disability insurance, you can make sure you still have income during your time of care and that you have income should you be unable to return to your previous level of activity.
- *Miscellaneous.* There are many other types of insurance policies that you can purchase to help you during your life, and they vary depending on where you are and what your needs might be (e.g., trauma insurance).

The more insurance you have, the more protection you have. However, this does come at a cost. You will need to add these payments to your expenses, so this means you will need to set aside more money than you may have anticipated.

There are some ways that you can manage the costs of your health care and other insurance policies:

- *Buy early.* The earlier you buy life insurance, the less costly it will be. Since you will be paying into the policy for a longer period of time if you start being a policyholder at thirty versus fifty, insurance companies will discount your rates. Find the policies that apply to you and sign up as soon as you can, long before you decide you will exit your company or your position.
- *Have larger deductibles.* The more you pay toward the services covered by your insurance policy, the less you will need to pay on a monthly basis. If this makes sense for your situation (i.e., you don't typically go to the doctor), then this is a way to help

offset your insurance costs. However, if you need to use your insurance more frequently, it may make sense to have lower deductibles and higher monthly payments.

- *Review your policies regularly.* It is helpful to look at your policies on a regular basis to see what's covered, what isn't covered, and what still needs to be covered in the future. Since changes can happen, you need to be certain you're still following the rules and that you're still in compliance with the limitations of the policy.

- *Find a group policy.* When you can buy an insurance policy as a part of a group (as many do when their employer offers insurance), you will be able to save some money. Look at alumni associations, professional organizations, and other affiliations to see if they offer you any reduced insurance rates.

- *Understand how to use your insurance.* While you might know how to use your insurance in many situations, if you're not clear how to use your insurance in its entirety, you may end up paying more for it than you need to.

- *See if you can be added to someone else's insurance.* If you have a spouse or a partner who has insurance, you might be able to join his or her policy. In those cases, it's often much cheaper for you while still offering you the insurance you need.

No matter what insurance you opt to purchase, make sure you are looking at all your options before making a final decision. The more you review the possibilities, the more you will see what makes the most sense for your particular situation.

Whenever possible, it can also help to get your entire family on a policy since that can help offset their costs, and it can help to ensure they are just as protected as you are during your retirement. (That said, adding people to a policy can be costly.)

184

DO YOU NEED MORE?

At the same time, the biggest question when it comes to insurance is whether or not you actually need as much as you think you do. For many people, they will overbuy insurance and then end up spending money they could have used for other activities or goals.

To help you determine if you need more insurance, think about the following questions:

- *What do you need insurance for?* Take some time to think about what kind of insurance you need and what you need that insurance for. For example, if you're a person with a chronic illness, you may need to have extra health care coverage to ensure your retirement isn't filled with medical bills.
- *How much can you spend now (and later)?* By looking at the money you have available for insurance, you might see how you can fit certain insurance policies in, but not all of them. Finding an upper limit to your insurance budget will help you make fiscally responsible decisions.
- *What does your insurance already cover?* Most people don't know what their insurance covers, so they buy policies that have more coverage than they need or they have two policies with very similar coverage. Take out all your insurance policies and see what you already have, and then cancel anything that is duplicated and add in anything that is missing.
- *What do your credit cards cover?* What you may not realize is that many credit cards will include some insurance coverage. It might not be a lot, but you may have some benefits of which you are not aware (i.e., travel insurance, rental insurance, property insurance, etc.).

The more you look at your insurance, the more you will know about whether you have enough coverage or if you need more.

At the same time, realize that insurance is something you may never use. You might simply pay into the policy and never have to utilize it. While this is the case, many people feel that having it available is much more reassuring than finding out you need it during an emergency.

ESTATE PLANNING

When you're readying yourself for your exit from a business, you need to keep something in the back of your mind: you are eventually going to die too. Though this is not the most uplifting thought for most, it is a reality, and it should factor into some of your decisions.

Estate planning is one of the areas in which your eventual demise plays a key role. In these plans, you are determining what will happen to the breadth of your estate, should you die before you exit your business or when you pass away after your retirement.

It can seem a little morbid for some, but there are many things that can go wrong with an estate, so planning ahead of time will help everyone, including your family.

WHAT COUNTS AS YOUR ESTATE

Your estate is the sum of your assets and possessions. During the course of your lifetime, you have amassed certain items, and when you die, they need to go to someone else. If you don't have a plan in place, you might have a few issues that can happen:

- *Fighting among loved ones*. Though you might not think your family would fight over your stuff after you die, it happens more often than you think. To settle these issues ahead of time, make sure you organize your belongings and let people know who gets what. Even if there are hard feelings, when you're still alive, at least you can talk things out and hopefully get things settled down.

- *Tax issues*. Because the transition of property to someone else will incur taxes, not preparing for this eventuality can lead to taxes your loved ones didn't expect to have to pay.

- *Business transition problems*. When your estate includes a business and properties associated with the business, it can become murky about ownership in the event of your untimely death. Some managers might feel the property is theirs, while others might not want to take on the responsibility, leaving the properties to languish.

- *Financial woes*. If there is no preparation for your estate, others might need to pay for things they didn't expect to pay for, which can cause distress for any grieving person. Instead, you will want to make sure you think about all these issues ahead of time.

In the process of working on planning your estate, you need to consider all the things that are a part of your life and all the things that will become a part of the lives of others when you are no longer around.

HOW TO PLAN FOR THE FUTURE

The more you plan, the less you will need to think about anything more than just enjoying your time outside of work. During your retirement years, you should be focusing on fun and not on the details that can get in the way of your enjoyment. To start to plan for your estate's transfer and transition:

- *Get help*. It never hurts to find a professional to help you plan your estate. This person can help you determine what you have, what you need to do, and how you need to organize the information in a way that will support your loved ones after you are gone. Often, this will be a person who will help you for a short period of time, and then you might meet up with him or her less often to update the documents, as needed.

- *Find out what you own/what you are responsible for.* Either with the help of an estate planner or on your own, start collecting a list of what you own. This will help you to see what needs to be cared for and how your life needs to be distributed and arranged ahead of time. Your list might include properties, possessions, childcare arrangements, leases, business ownership, stocks, investments, savings, etc.

- *Determine ownership transfers.* When you have a chance to see all you have in your estate, you can begin to see where you might want to assign new owners for these items. For example, you might know you want your house to go to your spouse or your child. Start writing out whom you think you will transfer ownership to, and then you can always change things if you decide otherwise.

- *Calculate taxes and set aside funds.* If you wait to do ownership changes and other transfers, you will need to find out what the tax costs will be. A professional who is well versed in estate planning will be able to help you estimate the costs. Once you know these costs, you can set the funds aside in an account that is dedicated to paying those taxes.

- *Transfer ownership now/share ownership.* While you might want to keep things in your name right now, it's going to be easier to share ownership with others to help make the transition after your death easier. The ownership will immediately transfer to that other person. Right now, make sure you share ownership of larger properties, allowing you to still be in control of the decision making but also ensuring the other owner will avoid any estate transfer issues in the future.

- *Document your decisions in a will and other forms.* You will need to write down all the decisions you have made and what they will mean in the future. It is ideal to have this written down in a will and have this notarized to ensure its authenticity. Copies of this document should be at your attorney's office, as well as in a safety deposit box and in a safe place in your home. You will want to make sure everyone knows where this document is and how it can be accessed in the event of your death.

- *Communicate with people.* Though you will have everything written down in a document, it's also a good idea to talk to others in your life about what you have done and what this will mean in the future for them. The more you can communicate now, the fewer surprises in the future.

Your estate may not be extensive right now, or it might be highly complex. Either way, you still need to consider estate planning as a part of your exit planning. The earlier you plan, the more you can set aside any necessary funds and the more you can begin to transfer ownership to ensure everything is in order.

TAX PLANNING

Most people would rather ignore taxes altogether instead of dealing with them. After all, if the tax issues aren't going to arise in their lifetime, why deal with them now?

However, it's best to take a proactive approach to any taxes you might incur, as many times those who are exiting their businesses to retire may not think about the bills that often come with taxes. As a result, they may not have set aside enough money to manage these needs, meaning they need to find ways to supplement their income instead of having the money available.

WHAT YOU NEED TO PAY

The main concern with taxes is that most people don't know what they need to pay. They aren't clear about what taxes will be owed or when they will be owed. Some of this will depend on the area in which you live, as well as the country in which you live.

For most, however, taxes will include:

- *Income-based taxes*. In many places, when you make money or you bring in more income than what it cost you, you need to pay taxes. Since you aren't drawing a paycheck, this doesn't mean you won't be paying taxes. Sometimes, the accounts from which you draw your income will incur taxes if you take the money out before a certain age.
- *Penalty fees*. Though you may not realize it, paying taxes late or not paying enough taxes may mean you need to pay fees. In some cases, you may not know about these fees until you are sent the bill, which can be frustrating and even financially devastating.
- *Property taxes*. If you own property, you will need to pay taxes on it. If you haven't thought about this fact, you might end up owing more than you realize, and since most property values will rise, the taxes will rise too.
- *Investment taxes*. Some investment accounts will incur taxes for withdrawals, as that is considered income. While the amount may not be a high number, it can become troublesome when your budget is already tight.
- *Capital gains tax*. If you make a profit on the sale of a non-inventory asset that was purchased at a cost amount lower than the amount realized on the sale, then you need to pay taxes (i.e., stocks, bonds, property, etc.).

While this is a long list, it is not an exhaustive list. Depending on your situation, you will need to think about what your potential tax situation may be.

This is why having a professional to help can be just what your exit plan needs to ensure you aren't surprised by an unexpected bill.

GETTING PROFESSIONAL HELP

Because tax codes change so frequently and you may not be able to keep up with all your tax responsibilities, hiring a professional is essential. They can help you navigate the processes and the documentation, while also helping you set up accounts to hold money for future tax payments.

Even though many people will not need to pay a lot in taxes as they get older, when you own a business, you can incur larger taxes during the sale of your company. Because you've taken in a large amount of money, this means you will also be making an income, which needs to be taxed in many situations.

When working with a tax professional:

- *Be honest*. The one thing that can cause troubles more than anything else in a tax-planning situation is dishonesty. Even if you're embarrassed by what has happened in your finances, you still need to be honest so the professional can help. Don't worry about being judged. They've seen it all. If you don't give them the information they need or you give them incorrect information, you might end up with a tax-planning strategy that isn't well suited to your needs.
- *Be communicative*. When you're working with a tax planner, it might be essential for them to know something about your financial history in a timely manner. Be sure you are

answering questions as quickly as you can, since your tax bill amount might depend on it.

- *Listen to the information.* As you work with a tax professional, be certain to listen to what he or she is telling you and what it means. This will help you better understand the steps you have to take now and in the future. Plus, this can also help you if you need to make decisions without a professional.

- *Pay fees/taxes on time.* Without a doubt, the most important part of your tax planning is to *make sure you pay your taxes on time*. Even when you're planning ahead for tax payments, be certain you are setting things up so your taxes will be paid on their due date, if not before.

- *Work on future strategies.* Focus on how you can prepare for future tax issues or problems. Though it would be nice to believe you will not encounter any issues, this is often not the case. Instead, you need to be ready to manage tax needs now so they don't surprise you later. Consider what will be taxed in the future.

- *Create a buffer for tax miscalculations.* Because tax rates change and you can't know for certain what you will or will not need when it comes to your taxes, it's a good idea to have a higher total for the money you will need available for taxes. Better said, save more than you think you need to save.

- *Have someone review your past taxes.* To help you spot any surprises ahead of time, it can help to have your old taxes reviewed by a professional. They will be able to see if there are any errors that need to be corrected and if there are any old tax payments that need to be made before they incur high penalties.

- *Stay organized.* As you get caught up with your taxes, you will want to create an organizational system that allows others to see what you have done and what you need to do in the future.

A tax professional can help you set up systems, but you need to ensure they stay organized.

- *Save money.* A professional can help you get the deductions you are entitled to and/or ensure that you don't expose yourself to fines due to items being claimed that you cannot claim.

Professionals may cost you extra money out of your pocket, but their experience can often help you avoid issues that could cost you more than just some extra cash.

RESOURCES

Have you considered and prepared the following in enough detail as part of your overall finances?	1 = Not Good 5 = Good
Retirement planning	
Insurances	
Tax planning	
Estate planning	

RETIREMENT PLANNING

In what level of detail have you considered the following as part of your retirement planning?	1 = Not Good 5 = Good
What will you do when you retire?	
How much money you will need the day you retire?	
What might others need from you when you retire?	
What do you already have in place?	
How will you fill the gap between what you have and what you need?	

FINANCIAL PLANNING

In what level of detail have you considered the following as part of your financial planning?	1 = Not Good 5 = Good
What investments do you already have in place?	
What is your investment success history?	
What investments will you make?	
How do you feel about risk?	
What help might you need?	

6
TRANSITION TO THE FUTURE

*Every day the increasing weight of years admonishes
me more and more, that the shade of retirement
is as necessary to me as it will be welcome.*

—George Washington, George Washington's farewell address

The future is going to be here before you know it—or it might already
be upon you. No matter where you are in the exit-planning process,
you have to think ahead in order to be ready. Just focusing on what is
happening today is not enough to secure your future.

Even though you're familiar with the buying process right now, it's
time to go into more detail about what this process looks like and
what you need to do to get the right buyer for your company—and
your future.

While it might seem as though things are out of your control at times,
the more knowledge you have ahead of time, the more prepared you
will be to successfully navigate these waters.

YOUR CLEAR PLAN OF ACTION

As a business owner, you already know the value of action. You know you need to do more and to be more than other companies out there. You need to act swiftly, you need to know everything about your company, and you need to be the person who is always ready to respond.

During this time of transition, a time when you're planning your exit and you're thinking about what might happen next, you need to have a clear plan. You have all the pieces of your plan right now, and here is how you can start to put it all together to ensure your success.

WHAT TO DO

The earlier you plan for your exit, the more you can accomplish. It's clear that the more a person prepares ahead of time, the more results they will see in the end. This is especially true when you're trying to move toward a time when you won't be working anymore.

Preparation during exit planning allows for:

- *More savings*. If you wanted to leave your job tomorrow, it would be impossible to do so, unless you've already been saving for years. When you exit your company, you want to have saved up for the expenses you will have in your new life. You can't necessarily count on selling your business for a price that covers all your expenses, debts, taxes, etc.
- *Less debt*. Just as in all parts of your life, the more time you take to plan ahead, the more time you will have to reduce your debt load. You can stretch out your payments, make them smaller, and ensure you aren't making things hard on yourself or others in the short term. It's much more manageable to reduce your debt slowly than to try to pay it all off at once.

- *A higher business value.* When you can work on a business development strategy over the course of years, rather than months or weeks, you will have a greater chance of driving up the value of your company. Doing this will help you get what your business is worth, and it will ensure your financial future is strong and stable.

- *A stronger team.* The more time you can spend on developing your team and preparing them for their new roles, the more confident they will be as well. You will have time to give them training that offers not only information but also the nuances of their positions in the company. You can also work on improving systems and actions while finding better team members to fill any existing or expected gaps.

- *A smooth transition.* When you're not running around and trying to make an exit work in a short period of time, you will have less stress to manage, and your team will have less worry as well. A smooth transition is more likely when you take small steps toward the eventual end goal, instead of having to quickly cross things off your list of things to do. This transition should be something that seems to happen naturally, not all at once, and it can take up to five years to execute.

- *Room for mistakes to happen.* While you may not expect any mistakes to happen or delays to occur, they will. You can plan for every eventuality and still have troubles. When you can make space in the strategy for this to happen, you will be able to manage these problems more easily. You will have time to assess the problem and create a practical solution. You will also have time to adjust your solution if it doesn't work the way you expected.

The more you plan now, the more you will benefit later. In addition, your team will also benefit from the transition, and they will see how you are supporting them in their future—not just leaving them to fend for themselves.

You've already learned in this book what you can do in order to create an effective plan for your exit. Now, you will learn more about how to plan for what happens after you leave.

WHEN TO DO IT

Planning ahead should start as early as possible and is not a single event that happens once. It is more like a series of discussions and actions, an ongoing conversation over time. Your business, financial and family circumstances, and possibly your priorities and preferences will change as you go through life, and it is important that any plans you make reflect those changes.

Reviewing your plans gives you a chance to keep an open mind about where you are going and enables you to communicate these changes with important people in your life, including family and staff.

Reviewing your plans should occur on a regular basis as well as when circumstances change. You may choose to review your plans regularly each year around your birthday, financial year-end, or around the new year. This will ensure that your plan remains relevant for you and that you remain on track to meet the end goals you have set. Circumstances that might prompt you to review your plans can include:

- change in your health
- change in family circumstances—marriage, divorce, birth, or death
- change in business performance or market you are operating in
- change in financial markets
- change in your team

When reviewing your exit plan, it is worth keeping the following in mind:

- *Secure documents.* Make sure you keep all your documents in a secure place where you can find them easily and they can be located by someone who might need to access them if you become incapacitated.
- *Annual review.* Decide on a time when it would be good to review your plans on a regular basis (e.g., around your birthday, the new year, or when doing your tax return).
- *Changing circumstances.* Be aware of other changes in your circumstances that may prompt a review of your planning documents earlier.
- *Legal documents.* Ensure with all legal documents, such as enduring guardian appointment or estate, that you check any specific requirements that might be required for reviewing or updating these documents (e.g., the type of witness or the need to complete a new form). It is always recommended that you seek professional advice in these circumstances.
- *Currency of your plan.* After any review, you may be happy to leave the plans as they are, or you may need to write new ones. If you leave them as they are, indicate this on the form by initialing them with the date. This will show the currency of your plans to people who may need to use the documents.
- *Verbal instructions.* If you have given people verbal instructions about your plans, which is not recommended, and you change your mind about these plans, make sure you contact these people and explain your current views.
- *Old copies.* If you have given people copies of documents related to planning ahead and you update or change these, make sure you contact the people, ask them to destroy old documents and online files, and give them current copies of documents and electronic files.

HOW TO PLAN WHAT HAPPENS NEXT

It might seem strange not to have an idea of what your life after your exit will look like. After all, you might have all your finances in order, but this doesn't mean you know what you will do—outside of being able to pay your bills.

What you might want to keep in mind is that you have some time to think about it as you're planning for your exit. This time allows you the chance to create the best possible life for yourself and your family.

Two final steps now remain. Get a buyer for your business and understand what you will do after you sell your business.

GETTING A BUYER

If only it were as simple as putting it out there that you want to sell your company, but it often isn't. At the same time, if your business is getting noticed, it will probably have a greater chance of being approached by an investor than the other way around. The use of a business broker can assist with getting you in front of the right buyers.

For your part, you do need and want to choose the buyer who will be the best fit for your company. This should be an investor who can:

- *Meet your goals and objectives*. During the process of selling your company, you need to have a certain set of objectives in mind. If you don't set this sort of system up, you will not be able to get what you want from the transaction. Have these nonnegotiable items listed out so that the buyer can see what your preferred terms are.
- *Agree to the best terms*. At the same time, you want to choose an agreement that will satisfy both of your needs. And that

might mean you need to compromise on some issues. In your terms of agreement, have a few things you will not negotiate on, but then leave some wiggle room so you can have a positive negotiation in which everyone gets something they want.

- *Understand the value of your business.* It's fair to say that everyone's business has value, but how much value is determined by what you can offer to the investor and to the market in which your business is already placed. To show the value of your company, you will want to talk to the investor about:

  - *How you create value for your customers.* If you're not sure how you can help your customers, you may not be helping them enough. While it might not seem important to you, the investor will see the holes in your plan. You need to make sure it's clear how your company offers value to your customers and how it will continue to offer value to customers.

  - *How you organize your company.* The more organized your company, the more an investor will be encouraged to become a part of the structure. Without a clear structure, your company will not necessarily be able to stay strong when you leave your position. Your company needs to already be set up as an entity that can survive change.

  - *How you sell your company's story.* You also need to come up with the story of your company and how it fits into the market. This might seem like a clever marketing strategy, but it's more than that. While you might be selling your company, you need to be able to sell your story to the person who will hand over the check. You need to appeal to their sensibilities and needs while also drawing them in emotionally.

- *Manage the tax consequences.* When you are selling your company, you will certainly have some tax consequences to manage (and to talk to your tax professional about), but you will also need to find a buyer who is aware of these issues. If they are aware, they can factor this information into their purchase.
- *Close the deal.* Of course, even if you find the best buyer in the world, if it's not a person who is willing to close the deal in the end, then it's not the buyer for you. If this is a person who has a history of not closing deals, then you may want to look for someone else to take on the responsibility of your company.

You are more in control of your company and of the sale than you might recognize. As a result, you need to be ready to qualify the people who are looking at buying your company and try to choose the buyer who is best suited for this unique transaction.

This might mean you need to say no to some offers and that you need to negotiate more with some people. Even if this is the case, remember you are arguing for your future and for your financial health.

WHO DO YOU WANT?

It's a personal decision when it comes to finding the right buyer for your business. While this might seem like a simple, logistic process, this is not always the case. To ensure you have chosen the right buyer, here are some things you can keep in mind:

- *Is this person qualified?* Even though you are not going to be around the company anymore, it does matter to the existing staff whether or not you have someone experienced at the helm. You need to make sure the person in the buying position is someone who can step in for you or that he or she has someone who can step in for you.

- *Does this person have experience?* While not every buyer is going to have experience in the specific industry you are in, he or she should have some sort of management experience and some sort of background in helping to build successful operations. It should not be someone new to the business setting.

- *Do this person have the funding to make the purchase?* Be sure to work closely with a legal team to guarantee that the funding you are promised is the funding you are going to get. Though it's difficult to get through a sale without finding this out early, the more professional support you have, the more likely you are to know when things aren't going the way they were meant to go.

- *How has this person done in the past?* Sure, the past is not always a predictor of the future, but when your company is successful, you want to make sure it stays that way, so you want to choose a buyer who has had success in the past and who will continue that record of results.

Though some people want to simply hand off their company to someone else, this is not always the best approach to a sale. Instead, you want to really think about whether this is a person who knows what he or she is getting into and what is ahead.

Someone who is knowledgeable will not only create success for your company in the future but is going to be a serious bidder and someone who is going to offer you the money your business is truly worth.

In addition, when you are selling a company, you need to think about the right choice for any family members who might remain. They should get a say in making the final call about who gets to be in charge. Don't leave them out of this conversation.

MAKING THE RIGHT CHOICE

There is no way to know if you're making the right choice, but there are plenty of ways to make the wrong choice. To ensure you're making the best choice for the health of your company and for the long-term success of the organization:

- *Understand the pros and cons.* When you're making a big decision, you need to carefully see both sides of the decision you are about to make. Think about all the benefits and identify all the negative aspects of the decision you want to make. Write this list down and review it several times to see if there are any new things that pop up in any column, especially when the new facts have the ability to change your mind.

- *Double-check your numbers.* Even though you might have the right numbers in front of you, you need to check and recheck these figures. You want to check what the sales total will be, outside of fees and taxes, as well as how much money you want to have in the end. You will want to look at the money you need for retirement and the money you want for other financial goals. The more you can look at these numbers, the more confident you will be about your final decision.

- *Ask for professional opinions.* Get outside insight into the decision you are about to make. Check in with your professional team to see if they have any questions or concerns, or if they see you are making the best possible decision. The more you can get advice from the outside, the more you will be able to see what is outside of your vision during an important, life-changing decision.

- *Include protective clauses.* As the legal documents are written up by your attorney or business broker, make sure you have some sort of protective clause(s) or stipulation that will allow you to back out of the deal in a short period of time. This will help you feel like you can change your mind, but it will also help you be ready to react if you get information after the sale has started.

- *Trust your instincts.* Though your gut may not seem as though it's a part of your professional team, your intuition often can sense things as being amiss before the facts reveal themselves. When you start to feel as though something isn't right, check everything again to see if you're missing something and whether you need to make adjustments or walk away.
- *Sleep on the decision.* During big decisions, it's a good idea to stop and think about every single detail and then give yourself some space to just sleep on the decision before you sign on the dotted line. Everyone needs to have a moment to breathe, and that includes you.

WHAT DO YOU DO NOW?

Once you've sold the business and all the value discussions are behind you, it's time to move forward. However, when you haven't been in this position before, you might not know what to do and what life looks like in this situation.

For some, selling the business doesn't mean they will leave their role immediately, so there is some relief in knowing this, but since you will be exiting eventually, it's time to think about what happens next.

WHAT DO YOU WANT TO DO?

During your life and during your leadership, you may not have thought much about what you wanted to do. Instead, you may have focused on making the right decisions for your company and the best decisions for growing the success of your company.

But what about you? What do you want to do?

There are many options, but here are the ones that many people consider first:

- *Retirement*. You might simply want to be done with your work and your position as soon as you sell the company. You might want to take the check and start doing all the things you haven't done because you've been at the helm of your business. You might travel, you might spend time with your family, you might start a new venture, or you might just sit around and enjoy your hobbies or watch television.
- *Advising*. Some people find they don't want to leave their working life so abruptly. They might choose to act as an adviser to the new investor or business owner. In this role, you might talk with the buyer about what he or she can do to ensure success, and you can be there to help with new directions as needed.
- *Mentoring*. Others may find they want to mentor people who continue to work in the company. This might include working with managers, with staff members, or with new hires to help them continue to see successful results.
- *New business*. You may also find you're inspired to start a new business, a new venture. For years, you may have been sitting on an idea, and now you will have time to put that idea into action. Or your previous business may have inspired a new angle or a new direction, which you can pursue now.

The question becomes: what do you want to do with your free time, and what do you want to do with your new life?

WEIGHING YOUR OPTIONS

It's typically a good idea to look at what the finish line for your career might look like long before you plan to exit your business. This will help you have more time to make better decisions instead of just making a spur-of-the-moment decision that doesn't end up serving you.

Here are some questions you can ask yourself to ensure you're making the best possible decision(s):

- *What do I want?* For most of our lives, we are told that our desires and our wishes are not as important as the wishes of others. However, when you are ending your career, it's time to focus on what you want and what you want to see happen next. Though you might have a little trouble narrowing down your options, remember that you can make decisions that only serve you at this point.
- *What do I like to do?* If you're having trouble figuring out what you want to do, then think about what you like to do when you're not in the office. As you reflect on this information, you may begin to see ways in which you can create a life for yourself that is in alignment with who you are and the kind of person you want to be now.
- *What have I missed out on?* When you've been building a successful business, you may have sacrificed more than you realize. Instead of thinking about all the ways in which you could be productive during your time away from work, think about what you have sacrificed to get where you were. Find ways to incorporate those activities into your new life.
- *What are my future goals?* The transition from business owner to retiree might not be as simple as you want it to be. You may need to have a little bit of structure in order to help you stay grounded and to help you stay motivated in your life. For some, setting some long-term goals can be helpful to get them from the sale of the company to the next phase of their life.
- *What resources do I have?* Of course, you have already considered the ways in which you might plan for your exit

from the working world, but you should also think about the resources you will have available to you. Though you might have set aside some funds, the more you can set aside, the more you can do.

When you have finally sold your business and you have moved out of the career path you forged for yourself, you need to make sure you're heading in a new direction. Even if you're not sure which direction that is, it's time to start thinking about it—as a part of your exit plan.

RESOURCES

Are you clear about what you will do after your exit?	1 = Not Good 5 = Good
Do you know what you want?	
Are you clear about what you would like to do?	
Have you considered what you have missed out on?	
Are your future goals clearly defined?	
Do you know what resources will be available?	

CONCLUSION

The future is upon you—or at least the idea of your future. You can see it in the distance, and you know that you have to prepare for it if you want it to be everything you hoped it would be. Though you might want to wait until you are certain about your future, others have shown that the more you plan now, the less you have to worry about the impact of unforeseen events (e.g., the economic downturn).

You can't stay in your role forever, and you need to find a way to exit that makes sense for you and that makes sense in terms of your financial goals and needs.

No matter what you choose, no matter where you are now, the more you plan ahead, the more you will achieve.

The plan is ready for you. The future is ready for you.

All you have to do is take the first step.

> *Someone's sitting in the shade today because*
> *someone planted a tree a long time ago.*
> —Warren Buffett

ACKNOWLEDGMENTS

My deepest thanks goes to my incredible wife, Davina. She has been a great encouragement and support to me in writing this book. She has also spent endless hours editing the content of this book. And, most of all, I want to thank her for her trust, love, hard work, and the beauty she has brought into my life. She is my best critic and motivator.

All books are collaborative efforts, and this one is no exception. Many people have contributed ideas, reviews, comments, and inspiration that have helped me turn ideas about exit planning into the reality of this book. Special thanks to my editors.

A big thank you to a client and friend, John Brain, for reviewing the first draft and writing the foreword to this book.

Thank you to my daughters, Linze and Chelsea, and son, Ashton, whom I hope will be inspired to realize that achievement in life is totally related to being strong in your faith.

REFERENCES

Australia. Parliament. Joint Committee on Corporations and Financial Services, Deborah O'Neill. 2013. *Family Businesses in Australia—Different and Significant: Why They Shouldn't be Overlooked.* Parliament of the Commonwealth of Australia.

Cooper, Chris, and Ohio Employee Ownership Center, Kent State University. *2013 Northeast Ohio Chapter of the Exit Planning Institute "State of Owner Readiness" Survey.* Accessed February 21, 2014. http://www.exit-planning-institute.org/userfiles/files/24A%20-%20State_of_Owner_Readiness_EPI_September_2013.pdf.

CoreValue Software. 2013. *Quantifying Transferable Enterprise Value in Small to Medium Size Enterprises (SMEs): The Value Driver Methodology.* Accessed February 21, 2014. http://corevaluesoftware.com/wp-content/uploads/White-Paper-Quantifying-Transferable-Enterprise-Value-CoreValue-Software.pdf.

Daniell, Mark, and Sara Hamilton. 2010. *Family Legacy and Leadership: Preserving True Family Wealth in Challenging Times.* Singapore: John Wiley & Sons (Asia) Pte. Ltd.

Department of Innovation, Industry, Science, and Research. 2011. *Key Statistics—Australian Small Business*. Parliament of the Commonwealth of Australia.

Dini, John F. 2012. *11 Things You Absolutely Need to Know About Selling Your Business*. CreateSpace Independent Publishing Platform.

Evans, Frank C., and David M. Bishop. 2002. *Valuation for M&A: Building Value in Private Companies*. Hoboken, New Jersey: John Wiley & Sons, Inc.

Exit Planning Institute. *Why Use a Certified Exit Planning Advisor?* Accessed March 7, 2014. http://www.exit-planning-institute. org/userfiles/files/Marketing-Member Recruitment/Brochures/ CEPA/CEPA_Online-1.pdf.

Finkel, David L., Stephen Wilklow, and Stephanie Harkness. 2010. *Building a Business, Not a Job*. USA: Bradstreet and Sons, a Division of New Edge Financial, LLC.

Hickey, Peter. *How to Increase Business Value and Prepare for Sale or Succession: Exit and Succession*. Accessed May 8, 2014. http://www. maus.com.au/Ebooks/Downloads/ExitSuccessionPlan.pdf.

Hickey, Peter. *How to Prepare Fast, Stunning & Comprehensive Business Plans*. Accessed May 8, 2014. http://www.maus.com.au/Ebooks/ Downloads/Business Plan.pdf.

Jackim, Richard E., and Peter G. Christman. 2006. *The $10 Trillion Dollar Opportunity*. Palatine, Illinois: Exit Planning Institute, Inc.

Jackim, Richard E. *Life After Business: Your Personalized Roadmap to Exit Your Business on Your Terms*. Accessed March 7, 2014.

https://www.exit-planning-institute.org/userfiles/files/
Downloadable_Content/Life%20After%20Business%20
Sample%20Report.pdf.

Lissner, Michael. *Sell Your Business Right the First Time.* Accessed
March 24, 2014. https://www.exit-planning-institute.org/
print_article.php?a=70.

McKinsey & Company. *Learn to let go: Making better exit decisions.*
Accessed February 21, 2014. http://www.mckinsey.com/insights/
strategy/learning_to_let_go_making_better_exit_decisions.

Mellen, Chris M., and Frank C. Evans. 2010. *Valuation for M&A:
Building Value in Private Companies.* Hoboken, New Jersey: John
Wiley & Sons, Inc.

MGI Business Solutions Worldwide. 2013. *Surviving Not Thriving: The
MGI Australian Family and Private Business Survey 2013.* Accessed
March 24, 2014. http://www.mgiaust.com/files/docs/mgi-family-
&-private-business-survey-full.pdf.

Mills, Jerry L. 2013. *The Exit Strategy Handbook: The Best Guide for
Selling Your Business.* United States of America: B2B CFO.

Nemethy, Les. 2011. *Business Exit Planning: Options, Value
Enhancement, and Transaction Management for Business Owners.*
Hoboken, New Jersey: John Wiley & Sons.

Patrick, Josh. *Seven Steps to Leaving Your Business in Style.* Accessed March
24, 2014. http://www.stage2planning.com/hs-fs/hub/13035/
file-447455788-pdf/docs/61313_61313_seven_steps_to_
leaving_your_business_in_style_403rev1.pdf.

Plener, Mike Boorn. 2013. *The 4 Pillars of Maximising Value.* Australia: Business Connector Publishing.

Pricewaterhouse Coopers. 2014. *Bridging the gap: Handing over the family business to the next generation.* Accessed May 8, 2014. http://www.pwc.com/id/en/services/assets/bridging-the-gap-2014.pdf.

Snider, Christopher M. 2013. *Exit planning is not what you think.* Accessed February 21, 2014. https://www.exit-planning-institute.org/members/index.php?section=resources&content=members-only-resources.

Snider, Christopher M. 2014. *Overview of Exit Planning Process.* Accessed May 8, 2014. https://www.exit-planning-institute.org/members/index.php?section=resources&content=members-only-resources.

Stage 2 Planning Partners. *Periodic Table of 56 Business Planning Strategies.* Accessed March 24, 2014. http://www.stage2planning.com/the-periodic-table-of-56-business-planning-strategies.

Stage 2 Planning Partners. *Basic Estate Planning.* Accessed March 24, 2014. http://www.stage2planning.com/stage-2-planning-basic-estate-planning.

Stage 2 Planning Partners. *Basic Retirement Planning.* Accessed March 24, 2014. http://www.stage2planning.com/get-your-free-report-on-the-basics-of-retirement-planning?bi_campaign=Brightinfo&bi_medium=referral&bi_source=app.brightinfo.com.

Warrillow, John. 2012. *Built to Sell: Creating a Business That Can Thrive Without You.* London, England: Penguin Books Ltd.

Wilcox, Jason N. *Exit: Selling Your Business For Maximum Price*. Accessed February 21, 2014. http://www.ws-ibank.com/files/Exit-Selling-Biz-for-Max-Price_WSCo.pdf.

Wilcox | Swartzwelder & Co. 2013. *Five Phase Process When Selling a Business*. Accessed February 21, 2014. http://www.ws-ibank.com/whitepapers/5-phases-company-sale-article.

Wilcox | Swartzwelder & Co. 2013. *How to Achieve Maximum Price?* Accessed February 21, 2014. http://www.ws-ibank.com/whitepapers/achieve-maximum-value-article.

INDEX

Printed in the United States
By Bookmasters